D0651485

THE JOYS AND SORROWS OF PARENTHOOD

Also by the Group for the Advancement of Psychiatry

Normal Adolescence: Its Dynamics and Impact
(formulated by the Committee on Adolescence)

The Right to Abortion: A Psychiatric View
(formulated by the Committee on Psychiatry and Law)

Drug Misuse: A Psychiatric View of a Modern Dilemma
(formulated by the Committee on Mental Health Services)

The VIP with Psychiatric Impairment
(formulated by the Committee on Governmental Agencies)

THE JOYS AND SORROWS OF PARENTHOOD

Formulated by the Committee on Public Education

GROUP FOR THE ADVANCEMENT OF PSYCHIATRY

CHARLES SCRIBNER'S SONS
NEW YORK

STATEMENT OF
PURPOSE

The Group for the Advancement of Psychiatry has a membership of approximately 300 psychiatrists, most of whom are organized in the form of a number of working committees. These committees direct their efforts toward the study of various aspects of psychiatry and the application of this knowledge to the fields of mental health and human relations.

Collaboration with specialists in other disciplines has been and is one of GAP's working principles. Since the formation of GAP in 1946 its members have worked closely with such other specialists as anthropologists, biologists, economists, statisticians, educators, lawyers, nurses, psychologists, sociologists, social workers, and experts in mass communication, philosophy, and semantics. GAP

5

envisages a continuing program of work according to the following aims:

1. To collect and appraise significant data in the field of psychiatry, mental health, and human relations;
2. To re-evaluate old concepts and to develop and test new ones;
3. To apply the knowledge thus obtained for the promotion of mental health and good human relations.

GAP is an independent group, and its reports represent the composite findings and opinions of its members only, guided by its many consultants.

The Joys and Sorrows of Parenthood was formulated by the Committee on Public Education, which acknowledges on page 7 the participation of various committee members and GAP Fellows in the preparation of this report. The current members of this committee and all other committees of GAP are listed at the end of the book.

ACKNOWLEDGMENTS

The Committee on Public Education was under the chairmanship of Peter A. Martin, M.D., when this report was formulated. At that time the committee also included the following members of GAP: Leo H. Bartemeier, Robert J. Campbell, Dana L. Farnsworth, Marion E. Kenworthy, James A. Knight, John P. Lambert, Norman L. Loux, Mildred R. Mitchell Bateman, Mabel Ross, Julius Schreiber, Robert H. Sharpley, Miles F. Shore, Robert A. Solow, and Kent A. Zimmerman. Dr. Farnsworth and Dr. Kenworthy, both past presidents of GAP, are now contributing rather than active members. The current chairman of the Committee on Public Education is Dr. Shore.

The committee wishes to express its appreciation to two GAP Fellows who aided in the formulation of this report, Dr. Jim Howard Earls and Dr. Michael McCulloch.

7

CONTENTS

PREFACE

The Committee on Public Education of the Group for the Advancement of Psychiatry (GAP) has prepared this report with the public in mind. We hope it will also be a useful reference for high-school and college courses in family living, and of value to those professionals involved with the interests of the general reader.

The composition of the Committee on Public Education spans the broad field of psychiatry, from young residents in psychiatry (GAP Fellows) to old-timers with fifty years of experience in clinical, administrative, or research areas. The full range of religious and ethnic backgrounds is included. The only common denominator is middle-class background.

This report represents private experiences and thus is not a scholarly research publication. Our observations, which have been culturally determined, may seem to be applicable only to dominant middle-class family patterns, but we are not stressing parent roles or variations of parent roles in the social system. There are many experiences common to all parents, whatever their socio-economic or cultural background. Generally, the process of parenthood does not differ widely. The focus is on parenthood as a period of life that offers the opportunity for continuing growth and development, not on the family as a structural unit.

This is not a how-to-do-it book. It does not present methods of applying principles to problems presented by children. It does apply itself to questions the committee thinks that parents should ask about themselves. What have I learned? How have I grown? What can I do now that I could not do before? What joys and pleasures am I experiencing in addition to enduring parenthood?

There have been many books written in which parent-child relations, their consequences and the processes involved, have been viewed almost entirely from the bias of the responsibility of the parent for the child. There is an overwhelming amount of material on the stages of child development, the needs of children, and the care of children. In contrast, relatively little has been written about the thought processes of parents. This report, then, centers on what it is to be a parent, on expectations for one's self instead of for the children, on the goals of an individual apart from the children.

Committee on Public Education
GROUP FOR THE ADVANCEMENT OF PSYCHIATRY

THE JOYS AND SORROWS OF PARENTHOOD

one

PARENTHOOD, A PERIOD OF PERSONAL DEVELOPMENT

Parenthood is a stage in the life cycle of the individual during which emotional growth and development continue. Though not often emphasized, this is probably the most enduring joy of parenthood. It is an active joy, derived from doing and becoming as opposed to the passive joy of receiving. The successful completion of this stage of life leads to increased ease in functioning and is indicative of positive mental health. Parenthood is more than a test of endurance at whose conclusion the most saintly of people may whisper, "And now, O Lord, may I go my way in peace?" To be prevented are the sorrow-filled experiences too often observed; to be avoided are the pitfalls of parenthood that ensnare the unprepared traveler.

Focusing on parenthood itself may seem to have an artificial quality to it, for the total family is the psychological field of study

15

and not its individual members. The needs of the parent cannot be separated from the simultaneous needs of the child and the responsibilities of marriage. Ideally, the needs of the child, of the parent, and of the mate mutually reinforce one another. Practically, however, these needs are to varying degrees in opposition, imposing frustrations and sorrows and forcing mutual adaptation. Often the literature appears to assume that the child, encountering his parents' attitudes as he grows and changes, interacts with a fixed quantity—the adult. Yet parenthood itself is a developmental process. Not only do inner and societal forces effect changes in the parent; the child too has an influence on the adaptation and personality development of the parents.

Parenting involves reliving one's own childhood experiences during each stage through which the child passes.[1] Parents and children develop together and interact with each other. To be able to feel what the child feels enlarges the parents' capacity for empathy in other interpersonal relationships.

Ideally, the parenting experience is relatively free of anxiety, guilt, and depression, and, both parents and children grow through this stage with successful resolution of their deep-seated ties and move freely to the next stage of their life cycles. Though the ideal may never be obtained, an understanding of the problems can help toward achieving a successful parenting and postparenting life.

DURATION OF PARENTHOOD

Parenthood has been described as a psychobiological process that ends only with the death of the parent.[2] To expect the reciprocal psychobiological involvements to end with the maturation of the children is a fallacy which is probably based on observations that children appear to outgrow their parents when they become parents themselves. Psychologically the stage of parenthood may never end.

However, life is not a static process, and an individual cannot remain forever an active parent. It is not healthy for him or for the child. Timely resolution of the relationship with freedom for each is the goal.

The healthy resolution of the parent-child relationship was expressed by Kahlil Gibran with his poet's insight into human nature:

Your children are not your children.
They are sons and daughters of Life's longing for itself.
They come through you but not from you.
And though they are with you yet they belong not to you.

You may give them your love but not your thoughts,
For they have their own thoughts.
You may house their bodies but not their souls,
For their souls dwell in the house of tomorrow, which you cannot
    visit, not even in your dreams.
You may strive to be like them, but seek not to make them like you.
For life goes not backward nor tarries with yesterday.
You are the bows from which your children as living arrows are
    sent forth.
The archer sees the mark upon the path of the infinite, and He
    bends you with His might that His arrows may go swift and far.
Let your bending in the archer's hand be for gladness.
For even as He loves the arrow that flies, so He loves also the bow
    that is stable.[3]

NEEDS OF PARENTS

Parents have personal needs that are in conflict with their need to be a parent, yet they often seem to be ignorant of their personal needs. One explanatory observation is that the instinct to preserve the species is strong in all living creatures and sometimes stronger than the need for self-preservation. Parents often feel their needs (physical or psychological) are secondary to the needs of the child. Unlike their children, they form part of the mainstream of life and have difficulty in being objective.

There are very strong cultural influences in the United States that value the care of the young above the needs of adults. Adults are viewed as being ideal, as "rugged individualists," as not having needs. Their behavior patterns are thought to be final, established, unchanging. Children and adolescents are expected to go through a number of developmental stages, but once they reach adulthood many people think their development is finished. The adult is supposed to stay basically the same in his thinking and needs and responses, at least until he reaches middle age and has to develop new directions for his life—and by this time his children are usually mature, so he is no longer an active parent. These views are not accurate. Parents are not just "vehicles" for the care of children. They are people, and parenthood is one phase in their total development as human beings, a development that never stops but continues from birth to death.

Development should be viewed from a broad perspective. The human personality does not stop suddenly at the end of adolescence and remain permanently fixed; it is constantly changing. The parent changes as he lives through critical life experiences and interacts with various people in his environment. He learns how to maintain an equilibrium by adapting to the forces that press on him from various directions at different times. Each new stage of life requires another adjustment of psychic forces and furthers the development of personality.

Parenthood should be a creative self-growth experience and not an onerous guilt-laden duty that saddles parents with full responsibility for any results that are less than perfect. Parents are not the only influence on their children. Social institutions also shape the personality of the child. Nor can parents devote all their resources to rearing their children. Part of their inner resources must remain available for their own continuing development as adults.

Some parents react negatively to the idea of not being totally responsible for the child's personality development. At first glance, this appears to be strange: since parents have been told for years that all their resources must go to their children and that they are to blame if anything goes wrong, one would expect them to appreciate relief from guilt. However, there are those who do not want to be relieved of guilt if the price that they pay is a loss of a sense of complete power and control over the child. If something goes wrong in the child's life, they prefer it to be their total fault rather than the partial influence of forces in the environment. If the cause is in the environment, they feel weak and helpless. Even the idea that they did something wrong may feel better to them than the fear that "No matter what I do, I cannot change the direction of my child's life."

Other parents cannot bear to feel guilt. They prefer to emphasize the effects of the environment and thus free themselves of all responsibility. They feel that they cannot live up to the idealized image of parenthood and stress that the external forces operating on their children are too strong for them to counterbalance.

On examination, in both these points of view the same thing has gone wrong. Anxiety about parental reputation and status has displaced an effective concern for the normal needs of the children and of the parents themselves. Parents have very strong needs, but these are covered up and denied, and come out in a distorted way in the life of the child. It would be much better for everyone—especially for the child—if parental needs were understood and met in a healthy way.

TRANSITION TO PARENTHOOD

Prior to the development of effective contraceptive devices, the first pregnancy usually followed so quickly after marriage that the major transition point in a woman's life was marriage itself. Today pregnancy is a more deliberate step, one that can be postponed until the couple feel economically, socially, and psychologically ready for parenthood. Getting ready, however, is not always a simple or easy matter. Education in American schools is notably deficient in subjects most relevant to successful family life: sex, home maintenance, child care, interpersonal relationships, understanding others. Preparation during pregnancy is confined to reading, consultation with friends and parents, and discussion between husband and wife. Often the wife receives a great deal of support from the physician who is caring for her during pregnancy, but his role is limited because he is usually not the physician who will care for the child and watch over its health and growth.

Many of the emotional aspects of parenthood are seen in miniature during pregnancy. In the early months a wife's chief concerns may be weight gain, vomiting, malaise, and possible loss of the baby—all fears relating to the new way in which her body is functioning. If she can accept, at the very beginning, the likelihood that bodily growth and development proceed naturally, she is less likely to be overwhelmed with concern over her child's growth. There are some women who "never felt better" than during pregnancy. Their physical health is good, their mental attitude is one of joyous anticipation. They feel fulfilled and never worry.

Later in pregnancy the wife may worry about whether or not the child will be perfect, whether she will lose her husband's love during the time she feels awkward and unattractive, whether she will be blamed for anything that goes wrong. Or she may revel in the attention and care she receives.

During this period the prospective father becomes more aware of his increased responsibilities and of the fact that his wife can no longer focus exclusively on him. He may experience real loss of her interest as she becomes more involved with her body and foetus.

The transition to parenthood is abrupt. One day husband and wife are alone; the next there is the sudden imposition of twentyfour-hour care and responsibility for a totally dependent infant. The mother's deep psychological and physiological functions help her to act as a mother, but though she receives meaning and gratification from her intimate relation with the infant, her need is relative and not absolute. The baby, on the other hand, has an absolute need for its mother—or for somebody who will perform the same functions she does. She gives and gives to the child, but the child cannot give her everything that *she* needs. The greater the degree to which sole responsibility for the newborn infant is placed on her, the greater is her degree of social deprivation. The husband can do much to help her care for the child and support her emotionally. Fathers have provided early care in many societies, and are doing so increasingly in the United States today.

Fathers also go through a new stage of development when a child is born. Fatherhood is a special manifestation of one's growth. The individual, after having achieved maturity, surpasses the growth of his own body and becomes able to produce a new individual. This means that as a man grows into maturity, he feels confident that his physical and emotional growth are mature enough so that he can create a new physical and psychological individual—his child.

A man's earliest security and orientation to the world are learned through experiences with his mother. These early experiences of the husband parallel those of the wife, and they are the origin of fatherliness as well as motherliness. The husband responds to his wife's needs and "mothers" her through her pregnancy. Soon after the birth of the child he develops a direct relationship with his offspring, enjoys the child's response to care, and feels pleased and fulfilled in being a good father.

It is difficult to adjust to being parents, and some writers look at parenthood only as a disruptive, upsetting "crisis" in a family. But rearing children is a normal human experience. People who become parents adapt to their new role and use it as a tool in their own personal development.[4]

PHASES OF PARENTHOOD

One useful way of looking at parenthood is to divide it into four phases: anticipation, honeymoon, plateau, and disengagement.

Anticipation. Some people have looked forward to parenthood from the time they were children, "Someday I will be a parent" was one of their first thoughts. "This is the way I would like to raise my children." When a man and woman marry, they start to think about becoming parents, and when pregnancy occurs they give special thought to how they will rear their children and what parenthood will mean to them. A great deal is known about the physical needs of mother and foetus during this time, but the psychological necessities for good mental health are much less well understood.

Honeymoon. After the baby has come, during the early months of parenthood, interpersonal adjustment and learning take place. This phase is similar to the first weeks and months of marriage, when the husband and wife have to learn to live closely with each other, and each adds a whole new dimension to the other's life. The attachment between parent and child is formed, and the members of the family learn new roles in relation to one another.

Plateau. This is the long middle period of the parental cycle. Most parents know that their children go through several devel-

opmental stages; they develop too, in ways that parallel those of
the children:

> The child is an infant: parents learn to interpret his needs.
> The child is a toddler: parents learn to accept growth and develop-
> ment.
> The child is a pre-schooler: parents and child learn to separate.
> The child goes to school: parents learn to accept rejection and still
> be supportive.
> The child is a teen-ager: parents begin to rebuild their lives.[5]

During the earliest months of a baby's life, the parents' most
difficult problem is finding out what the baby is trying to tell
them. The infant is physically helpless, and his emotional involvement with his parents determines much of his future emotional
health. This has been called the period of "trust." [6] The infant
needs to establish confidence in his mother and in his environment, because this is a necessary foundation for all his future development. The parents need to establish confidence in their ability to understand the infant's needs and to respond to those needs
not only adequately but with ease and affection. They need to develop the capacity for empathy—understanding and joining in the
infant's feelings. The ability to do this, which contributes greatly
to both parent's and child's interpersonal relationships, has its be-
ginnings in infancy.

When the infant becomes a toddler he begins to assert his independence, his first ideas about his own individuality, and will-
power. This has been called the period of "autonomy," since it
represents the earliest development of self-reliance and self-control.[7] The parents, who have until now had a helpless infant, must
accept the child's growth and begin to "let go," while the child
vacillates between dependence and independence.

At the pre-school period, parents often do not realize that separation anxiety can be as difficult for them as it is for the child. Parents are told to allow the child to assert himself, to explore, to show initiative; but at the same time they have to set limits and be present when the child needs them. They can become confused and frightened because the child no longer seems to need them so much. The child imitates them, and when they are able to accept this initial separation, so can he.

The school-age child needs to fit into his peer group. He moves away from his parents, often ignoring them. This is the time of "industry" or "work completion," when he learns to win recognition by producing things and performing tasks set by teachers or peer-group members. His social life gives rise to an inner discipline, and he may develop a strict conscience in his attempts to control his aggressive and sexual drives. During this time parents must learn to give support in an unobtrusive manner, without feeling hurt, disappointed, or angry. They must respect the child's feelings and his pride. Parents who need reassurance of the child's faithfulness are the unhappiest people in the world. They experience the child as an extension of themselves and are more outer directed in their values. They have, so to speak, put all their eggs in one basket. If the child is considered highly by other people, they experience a rise in self-esteem. If the child exhibits limitations in achievement, the parent feels a fall in self-esteem. If the child is successful and moves away from the parents through his successes, the parents experience rejection and a loss of self-esteem. Separation anxiety needs to be overcome by both parent and child.

In the adolescent's struggle to his own identity, the peer group often becomes more important than the parents (or any other

adult authority). Parents may find it difficult to confine themselves to specific important issues, to respect the young person's
feelings, to avoid constant criticism or disapproval. In order not to
undermine morale and relationships, teen-agers need to be encouraged to establish separateness from the parents.[8] Parents must
now start to rebuild their own lives. Success in their own self-development makes it possible for them to give support and help as
needed without intruding on the adolescent's growth, and to relinquish control gradually as their child becomes more mature.

The accelerated rate of change in our society has made the ad-
justments of teen-ager and parents even more difficult. Fundamental changes such as urbanization and geographic mobility
have affected the nature of society's institutions, including the
family. There has been a shrinking of the size of the family from
the extended family of many relatives of an earlier day to today's
relatively isolated nuclear family. The generation gap, or genera-
tional differences, in cultural values, knowledge, and outlook tend
to be magnified. If parents look only to their own experiences for
guidance in understanding their teen-ager's needs, they are almost bound to encounter frustration, bewilderment, and disappointment. As a consequence of being exposed to the concerns of
their adolescent children, many parents have undertaken an ago-
nizing reappraisal of a number of their own attitudes and beliefs.

Disengagement. This stage leads up to and includes the end of
the active parental role, which is generally considered to be the
time of the child's marriage, although this varies greatly and may
in reality never end. Some people try to force their active role as
parents all their lives or are forced to by life circumstances (such

as having a retarded or physically handicapped child) even though they wish termination of the responsibility.

How Parents Grow

The goal of adolescence is maturity—both physical and psychological. As we have seen, a person's emotional and psychological growth does not come to a stop at the age of twenty; the person continues to grow and develop as a human being. When the individual is physically mature enough to have a child and psychologically mature enough to gratify both the child's needs and his own, he is ready to become a parent.

People do not grow by advancing only in a straight line, with never a backward glance. More likely, they grow in spirals. Starting in the present, they move ahead a little, gain new knowledge or understanding, then circle around, consider what has happened before, and integrate the old with the new. The past and the future are always acting on each other. Recognition of this pattern can prevent unnecessary anxiety.

Parenthood is a big step forward that requires a great deal of reconsidering of the past. In the process of learning to be a mother, a woman re-experiences what happened to her when she was being mothered. As she cares for her child, she may feel satisfied that she is taking good care of the child and develop into an even more capable person; or she may feel frustrated and unhappy about her lack of ability and slip backward to a lower level of functioning. Just as the infant gains confidence and self-esteem through a good mother-child relationship, so does the mother.

Even though one does not consciously remember all that hap-

27

pened in childhood, everyone has a host of feelings about it—whether the family was happy or not, whether there were confidence and acceptance and love, or whether the predominant feelings were rejection and insecurity. As the parents care for their own children, many of these old feelings come up again. This is normal, the way it is supposed to be. In each period of the child's growth parents rework what happened to them many years ago. They turn back in the spiral. Hopefully, they then return to a higher point; most people do. Those who cannot resolve the conflicts fall back to a lower level of functioning or show symptoms of mental illness.

The child acts as a mirror for his parents. They see themselves in the child. If his behavior expresses positive aspects of the parents—if he is loving, happy, intelligent, creative—his parents feel that these qualities are reflections of themselves. They feel satisfied with what they have done thus far and more able to go on successfully. When the child expresses negative aspects, the parents feel shocked and threatened.

All children, for example, whine and fuss occasionally. The books on rearing children indicate when this is likely to occur, how much is normal and how much is a symptom of personality problems, and how the child should be treated in order to get him through the "fussy stage" with lasting gains but no lasting damage. What has not been dealt with adequately is the effect of this on the parents. For parents to be upset is natural. "My child must have learned this from me! Do I really whine and complain like that?" Some parents will deny that the child could possibly have learned this from them. Others can use the feelings of shock and threat to change and develop into more mature individuals.

The child's idealization of his parents increases their self-esteem. This is seen in the father's response to the admiration of his son or flirtation of his daughter, the mother's pleasure at her daughter's femininity and her son's love. But many people have never solved completely the conflicts they may have felt over their sexual attachments to their parents; they may still feel concerned and guilty about these. When a child reaches that period, the parent works through his old conflicts again, this time from the viewpoint of an adult. A successful relationship with the child may help the parent to come to a greater acceptance of himself and the nature of human sexuality.

Every person carries with him not only those things that have happened in the past but also those that he hopes will happen in the future. Becoming a parent reactivates many old conflicts and many new hopes of which the individual is barely aware or not at all aware. Parents rarely ask themselves, "What can we do to rear a child who will become the kind of adult we and society value? What is the best way for us to integrate our role as parents with all the rest of our roles as adults?" Yet they operate under such pressures, react to them, and are influenced by them. As indicated earlier, pressures that peak at late adolescence, at the time for separation between the parents and their children, are heightened in a society experiencing rapid change.

EXPECTATION AND DISAPPOINTMENT IN PARENTHOOD

two

People do things for many different reasons. Their past experiences, their basic needs, the society around them—all play a part in motivation. Psychologists now know a great deal about the forces, particularly those from the past, that *drive* people, but less has been learned about the expectations that *lead* people. Expectations are involved one way or another in all behavior. At suppertime, we decide what to eat partly on the basis of being hungry, but also on the basis of an expectation of how a particular food will taste. When our expectations are realistic, we leave the table with a satisfied feeling. But sometimes we have overestimated the cook or the dish and end up hungry and disappointed.

Expectation involves such important aspects of personality as faith and hope—ingredients essential to human life. But hand in hand with expectation goes a certain amount of disappointment. The relationship between them affects the feelings that parents have about themselves and their children and influences how they act toward their children. Most of all, it determines how parents feel about having been parents as they look back in their later years.

The expectations that people have about parenthood are as varied as are most things about human beings. Many of them are conscious. Most people, if asked what they expect parenthood to be, can say a good deal about it. At the same time, many are partially or completely unconscious and come out only in parents' attitudes and behavior. The unconscious expectations, because of their unrealistic elements (and there are always some of these), may take a long time to be modified by the way things really are. The more parents can unravel these unconscious expectations, the more they can fit their expectations and their actual life experiences together.

COMMON EXPECTATIONS

The earliest and perhaps most critical expectation of all is that of birth itself. Since no one knows what one is producing, emotions boil up to a very tension-filled moment until the product becomes obvious. The common experiences around the birth of the baby are joyous ones for both the nuclear and the extended family. Overestimation of the love object is seen here to an extreme. Around this particular critical point, the relationship of parents to child is often made or broken. Many children are either highly accepted or highly rejected, to the extent that this attitude may continue for years.

Another expectation is that children will be an extension of their parents' lives, particularly the highly valued aspects. They express the parents' faith that life is worth continuing and that there is something in their own lives that should be carried on. Most parents hope that their children will have the experiences that have made them happiest and will show the attitudes and abilities that they are proudest of in themselves. They want to take pride in their children and feel that through their children their lives are extended into future generations. The child is thus a form of immortality and a contribution to the progress of mankind.

This may not always be ideal from the child's point of view. Children struggle to grow up, be themselves, separate from the parents. Overly proud parents, or those who push to extremes the similarities between themselves and their children, may make the child's separation more difficult. Disappointment sets in when the child does not fulfill the parents' expectations. Not all baseball fans' children are natural athletes; beautiful mothers have awkward daughters. A parallel, and sometimes even more difficult, situation occurs when the parent communicates the idea that because he cannot do a particular thing, neither can the child.

Most children, sooner or later, surprise their parents by turning out to be only themselves in some important respects, by having some qualities uniquely their own, different from either parent's. The ensuing disappointment varies in its severity and in the degree to which parents are aware of it. Humor, irritation, a sense of sadness, may be parts of a psychological process by which parents come to terms with the disappointment. The parent who cannot see his child in any terms except as an extension of himself may reject the child or keep up continual, futile attempts to change him. Both the disappointment and the way it is handled may be unconscious; the parent may never connect his feelings and actions with his unfulfilled expectations, unless he happens to give it serious thought. This process of high hopes followed by ensuing disappointment sets up a mechanism for feelings of loss of self-esteem and depression.

Parents' misconceived expectations include the idea that children offer them a second chance. Besides hoping that children will carry on their best qualities, fathers and mothers often expect their children to make up for what they feel is lacking in themselves.

Everyone has regrets. There are always personal failings that haunt one, deficiencies, insecurities, and frustrations that one wishes one could correct. The father who attributes his life's unhappiness to lack of education will do anything to see his son get a college diploma whether the son wants it or not. The mother whose life has been clouded by financial worry wants her daughter to marry a "financially successful" man and have an easier life than she had. In so doing, the focus is on one factor and all other considerations are eliminated. Parents who grew up without brothers and sisters, or without close ties to their parents, sometimes want a large family full of companionship and friendly activity. The youngest in large families, distressed by fighting, jealousy, and lack of privacy, look forward to having one or two children and a peaceful, noncompetitive family life.

Some expectations may be largely fulfilled, may work out the way the parents hoped, and disappointment kept to a minimum. More often, especially if the expectations mean a great deal, the reality falls short in some way, and parents have to cope with definite disappointment. Here the wound may be double. If children fall short in areas where the parents are satisfied with themselves, at least the self-satisfaction remains; but if the child fails to make up for an earlier frustration, it is a second blow to the parents. The danger of this kind of double disappointment is that acceptance of the children on their own terms is then extremely difficult.

A common reaction to the threat of disappointed expectations is to pressure children to achieve. Some parents push scholarship; others, athletic prowess. Society in recent years has reinforced such pressure. The post-sputnik anxiety about American schools has resulted in breakneck acceleration of the curriculum. Through Little League, Pee-Wee hockey, and Pop Warner football, children may be coerced into early professionalism and fierce competition. The result is the death of childhood and a generation made up of prematurely sophisticated, harassed children, for whom learning and sports are completely serious business, devoid of joy in the activity for its own sake; and of drop-outs, who remain permanently unsophisticated in reaction to expectations they cannot possibly meet.

Another expectation that parents may have is that in normal family life there is no trouble. The logical extension of this is that when there is trouble, someone or something has gone wrong. Upheaval is resented as an intrusion on the peace and quiet that are believed to be "normal"—in spite of the fact that peace and quiet are often disrupted. Many people think that family life should by its nature consist only of love between parents and children which results in respect and appreciation. An average day is supposed to be one in which any moments of disagreement or ir-

35

ritation are quickly resolved by talking, by good humor, without high-pitched emotional involvement. Rivalry between brothers and sisters is thought to be superficial and leavened by basic loyalty and companionship. Parents are supposedly mature and selflessly involved with children through their love for each other and their desire to do the best they can for the children.

This view has been reinforced by the deluge of writing advising parents how to do better by their children. The underlying assumption of most of this literature is that family life ought to be peaceful, and if there is upheaval something has gone wrong which can (and should) be corrected by more effort or wisdom on the part of the parents. The amount of parental guilt and anxiety thus generated is incalculable. It is unfortunate and ironic, because there are scientifically sound but rarely discussed reasons why family peace is *not* always possible, because of the very nature of parenthood. The achievement of relatively peaceful or tension-free states is possible, and these times are deeply appreciated by children and remembered fondly when they become adults as the happy, carefree days of childhood. There is, moreover, a positive value of frustration—a certain amount of tension is a stimulant to growth. Certainly some conflicts or periods of turbulence in family life are significant and need to be examined. However, parents need a double awareness: that family life, by its very nature, cannot be wholly without some rough spots; and that not every stormy occasion is a forerunner of an oncoming destructive tornado.

REACTIONS OF PARENTS TO CHILDREN

One basic difficulty for parents is that children are childish, and their immaturity is a powerful stimulus for the parents to react in a childlike manner in turn. This may seem odd, since children pattern themselves on the maturity of their parents. They tend strongly to imitate and identify with their parents, or at least with many of their parents' outstanding traits. As in physics, where every action calls forth an equal and opposite reaction, so in child-parent relationships the child acts as a magnet to draw the parent into the orbit of immaturity.

The simplest example is the way adults bill and coo and make fools of themselves over infants. Although this foolishness is enjoyable, there is also an edge of disapproval, for the adult has temporarily accepted a return to childhood behavior, and what appears to be childishness makes other adults nervous.

Deeper and less obvious examples of return to earliest behavior are more complex. Consider the reaction of both parents to the infant in the earliest stage of life. Some infants are placid and others tense and irritable, but all are an around-the-clock responsibility. They require care, attention, and concern, and having to supply constant and life-sustaining care is a very special drain on both parents, physically and emotionally. In our society the mother usually has the chief responsibility for the infant's care; her capacity to sense the baby's needs and respond appropriately depends on several things. Fathers, other members of the extended family, and mothers' aides or substitutes also parent the young. Important for all of them is the ability to empathize, to feel things as if they were the child. Doing this involves another kind of remembrance in which they are tuned in to the touch, the smell, the appearance of the child. They feel its distress with themselves and enjoy its comfort and satisfaction. How they feel depends to a great extent on their own early experiences. If these were unpredictable and associated with physical discomfort, they will be upset by the child's distress, awkward in attending to its needs, and unconsciously envious of its comfort. They may be too anxious to pace themselves according to the infant's schedule. If their own early experiences were pleasant, on the other hand, they will be more able to re-create with the baby the good experiences that they themselves had. They will feel that its discomfort is manageable and not overwhelming, and they will enjoy the baby's change from distress to peace which results from their care.

The temporary excursion back to childhood set off by the baby's needs may have both pleasurable and painful consequences. Since no infancy is perfectly blissful or without periods of distress, every mother carries some unpleasant reminders of her childhood and experiences some anxiety when she slips into childhood with her infant.

Moreover, though infantile demands can be met in the short run, they recur. The only solution to the baby's constant demand for care is for him to mature from infancy to childhood and then to adulthood. There are times with even the easiest baby when both parents have to walk the floor in shifts. Though desired, peace is not always possible. If parents believe that it is, and that therefore they have failed, their morale sags. The mother's self-esteem particularly is tied up with infant care. If things go badly, she may become anxious, defensive, or resentful of the child, herself, her husband, or some other convenient object.

Although the mother's reactions are the most obvious, since she is directly in contact with the child, the father is involved too. The relationship between husband and wife is readjusted when they become parents, and each must establish a relationship with their child. Even when the balance is re-established, there are ups and downs. For instance, when the baby has colic, the mother feels she may have done something wrong, she must spend more time with the baby, taking it to the doctor, changing its formula, holding it, worrying about it. Somehow the baby always demands the most attention at dinnertime, when the husband's needs are greatest. Her concerns for the baby make it harder to take care of him. The husband, although concerned about the baby, may feel neglected and find fault with his wife about some other issue; she, feeling doubly criticized, experiences even more anxiety and guilt. Everyone feels that something is terribly wrong. What is really wrong is in the original expectations. Husband and wife expected that their life together could be forever peaceful, that any disturbance is abnormal, that anything less than perfection is proof of their failure.

Problems due to the child's dependency are most common early in infancy, but they are present as long as one is living with children. As children grow, their problems may involve parents in other forms of regression. From ages two to four, for example, the issue is control of aggressive energy. At that age children become very active and intrusive. They get into everything, and they push to see how much of the world (including their parents) they can manipulate and control. Their means of attempting control include tantrums, saying "no," and going off on their own in certain limited but provocative ways.

The parents' task in this is to help the child control *himself,* his anger and his behavior. The temptation is to be drawn into the excitement of the child's provocation and respond in kind with a fury that is rationalized as the only possible way to control the child. Psychiatrists and psychologists have long known that aggression and violence can generate a special kind of excitement and longing to participate. Experience with the effects of mass communication and with riots has recently helped the public to understand this phenomenon. At home there is a fine line between the judicious use of force to control unreasonable behavior and the gratification of indulging in uncontrolled rage at the out-of-hand child. The line is as difficult to draw there as it is in the confusion of a campus riot.

The sense of having won but lost that overtakes the enraged parent when a furious spanking is over reflects his awareness that a regression to the child's own level has taken place. For all parents, it is extremely hard to deal with a provocative, out-of-control toddler without responding in kind. However the parent responds, the provocation itself disrupts the expected peacefulness of family life. The disruption is an inevitable part of growing up and not a sign that something has gone wrong.

There is another kind of childishness that draws parents into childlike types of feelings and behavior. Many children are fascinated by their own and their playmates' bodies; they enjoy the power of forbidden words and love to talk about toilet functions. Some parents are frightened and repelled by this fascination, even though they may be aware that this is a natural stage in development and should be managed without undue alarm. Other parents are as delighted as the children and use their understanding of the "modern" approach to dwell upon body functions and increase the child's excitement by their own interest. Many parents experience a combination of disgust and fascination, as determined by their own childhood experiences when encountering these areas of growth and development. The forbidden excitement and guilt that the parent felt as a child are reactivated by his child's discovery of his body, and the result is a loss of the mature perspective that would help the child to master his obsession with body functions.

The tendency of adults to replay old fears and conflicts with new characters, though this is often unwitting, disrupts the peace of family life with bewildering frequency. Since children show physical and temperamental features of both sides of the family, they are easily identified with significant people in the parents' lives—one of the grandparents or a sibling. It is usually a relative about whom there is substantial emotional conflict, and the conflict is displaced onto the child and the old scenario re-enacted.

A physician's eldest daughter was sensitive, high-strung, and emotional, like her grandfather. Her father had always hated and feared his father's volatility and temper tantrums, which he regarded as evil and self-centered. He had coped with his father's emotional demands by being a hard worker and helper and by a keen sensitivity to his moods. He could forestall his father's rage by anticipating his demands and being a model son. His attitude toward his daughter was suspicious and critical. Although he tried at times to appease her, he more often showed the resentment and anger that had been buried because of his fear.

Since such reactions are hard to understand on the surface, parents often feel very guilty about them. If they stop and think "Whom does the child remind me of? What conflicts out of the past am I replaying?" they can often get a clue to the source of the difficulty.

A variation of this is the hurt of not seeing any aspects of one's self, one's mate, or one's parents in the child. This happens more often than has been noted in the literature.

It should not be thought that all parental expectations are doomed to failure. Just as frequent are instances of fulfillment of expectations and instances where the child goes far beyond the wildest expectations of the parents. Talents and abilities not noted in the parents often are shown by the child. This may be in such areas as scholastic ability, musical ability, artistic talents, or athletic prowess. Or the child may be one with a particularly happy disposition whose joy in life is a pleasure to observe. With these children, fulfillment of parental expectations or gratifications beyond their fondest hopes lead to elation and parental confidence. The parent feels he has done a more than satisfactory job. Sometimes this self-satisfaction is well earned and well deserved. Sometimes there is an element of luck involved, because there are always a number of uncontrollable factors present in the rearing of children.

It has been noted that during the early years of verbal communication it is pure pleasure for the parents to participate in the child's baby-talk, to observe the evolution of his language and how much more he knows than they expected.[1] Parents respond to the spontaneous expressions of the child with a sense of gratification, as a lucky extension of themselves. Later, when the child's individuality emerges, forecasting its definite contours, that communication becomes less understandable by empathy and disappointments ensue.

In current American culture, parental expectations of adolescents seem to bring the most parental disappointments. Here expectations of significant people in the adolescent's current environment also play a part in determining his sense of identity as well as his behavior.[2] The parents, the peer group, and the community all indicate their expectations of him for success or failure. Confusion lies in that the expectations of one may be contrary to those of the others. Peer groups stimulate the devaluation of parental authority, leading many parents to confuse the rebellion in manners for a rebellion in morals, with the result that parents expect the worst. Some parents expect continuing dependence, others expect premature independence. When both expectations are present simultaneously the adolescent is confused. A parent may expect independence in money matters but continuing dependence in making other decisions.

Around the issue of going to college, some parents expect the adolescent vicariously to accomplish for them or successfully to compete for them. Rebellion against such pressures again causes some parents to expect the worst. It is helpful if parents do not lose faith in themselves or in the child's potential. They should expect the adolescent to behave consistently with society, to develop a reasonable degree of independence, to make educational and vocational choices within his competence and his interests, and to develop a healthy social and sexual identification. Optimistic expectations are often an expression of the parent's trust in himself, whereas pessimistic expectations may be feelings of distrust of one's self projected onto the child.

The Dilemma of Parenthood

The parent may be the best kind of person he can be, but the final product is not entirely within his control, no matter how much of his life he devotes to the children. This might be called the "True Dilemma Theory of Parenthood." There is such a thing as a true dilemma—a situation that has no solution, in which, whatever choice is made among those available, the end result may be less than desired. Should the result turn out to be better than the parent wished, a fortunate turn of events, something beyond parental control may have been the decisive factor giving it the final direction. There are no simple formulas on how to rear an individual child to reach the parents' expectations. There is no how-to-do-it recipe book. Many factors are involved in rearing children, some outside the parents' control. Even at a single point in time, with a small problem that appears to be simple, there may be no "right" or "good" answer—merely a choice. Choices are made with no certainty that good consequences will outweigh bad ones. Parents care terribly whether the consequences are good or bad, but the intensity of their wishes does not influence the outcome.

In a case that illustrates this point a teen-age boy resisted continuing his religious education. He attended parochial school after his secular schooling. The work was difficult for him; he did not keep up with the rest of the class and he skipped classes. He was the type of child who wanted to please his father so he went to the school building; but he could not stand the embarrassment of being inadequate in his classwork. Instead of going to class he wandered through the building, engaging in friendly conversations. His father was continually pressuring him, hoping to see some of his own ambitions realized through the boy. After a long period of struggle, the disturbance created in the home was more than the mother could stand, and she sought help. A detailed examination of the multiple factors in the home led to a recommendation that the boy be allowed to withdraw. A dilemma then faced these parents. If they allowed the boy to stop his parochial schooling they were not only giving up their hopes that he would become a scholar but were also afraid that a pattern of dropping out would be established in his character. If they forced him to continue, there would be daily confrontations and disturbances in the parent-child relationship. There was no good choice, and they decided to take the path of least parent-child friction, to allow him to grow up into what he was and not what they wanted him to be. In light of this decision, the ending of the story is ironic. At parochial school one of the teachers who took a personal interest in the boy chided him for dropping out. He proposed that the boy come into his current events class, which was an advanced class for the brightest students, without having to attend the other classes. This arrangement was an individual choice by a teacher who liked teaching and was made without approval of the administration. The boy respected the teacher, wanted his approval, and accepted the conditions. It should also be noted that the boy knew that he was not being forced to continue and could make a choice. Human lives consist of many such unexpected turns of events.

INNER PEACE FOR PARENTS

A distinction should be made between expectations and rewards. Parents may feel that they deserve a reward from the process of being a parent, and may be disappointed if they do not get it. It is not only children who need to be loved; the need for parents to be loved by children should also be recognized. Creative literature is filled with stories of ungrateful children, as in *King Lear*.

Enjoyment of the child as he is and a realistic appraisal of what can be expected from him offer the parents opportunities for gratification rather than disappointment. Inner peace, if this is the parents' expectation, comes from development of the father's or mother's own inner resources rather than from the child's fulfill-ment of parental expectations. Ideally a parent should strive to be-come as free from his own childhood-determined expectations as possible, so that there will not be too great a discrepancy between his expectations from children and the way the children really are.

three THE PSYCHOLOGY
OF VALUES

Establishing Parental Values

It is probable that for parents the area most accompanied by inner uncertainty and insecurity is that which deals with establishing a moral climate in the home. Among the reasons for this is that the inner values of the parent are affected both by the experiences of each new stage of growth and development, and by changes in society's values. The pressures to change old, established values are great, but these are deeply embedded in the personality and anchored in strong feelings.

Another source of confusion is the conscience, or superego, for "conscience" has different meanings to different people. The religious person may claim that conscience is the voice of God and even state that it must always be obeyed. A cleric may state that conscience is the human capacity or instrument for hearing what God says but that human capacity can at times be ignorant, blocked, and misinformed. Others consider conscience as a set of values transmitted from one generation to the next. The process of transmitting these values also transmits prejudices so that the adult needs constantly to re-evaluate and reassess his values in the light of new experiences and information.

Another difficulty in establishing a stable, enduring, easily transmittable set of values is the tendency not to practice what is preached. Parents tend to communicate double messages to children. If what the parent says and does is consistent during the child's formative years, a conflict within the conscience will not be evident. If in addition this is consistent with what the child perceives in his experiences with his culture, the result will be a stable, well-balanced person. However, no culture is free of contradictory and conflicting value systems and contrary activities. It is with such conflicting forces that parents must work to establish and maintain their own set of values before they can function adequately in the transmission of values. It is necessary to recognize that a two-way system (even though weighted in one direction) exists in that moral values are also transmitted from children to parents. The child's moral dilemmas at each stage of his development stimulate a reworking of the parents' position about each issue.

Some of the inner values that the parent needs to establish firmly have already been discussed: the value of lifelong personal growth and development as giving an important meaning to life; the value of successful separation of self and child with two equal and adequate adults resulting; and the value of realizable expectations for oneself in place of expectations from one's children. In addition, integrity, wisdom, and a feeling of kinship with mankind should be achieved and maintained through the parenting experience.[1] From the empathic experiences with children the parent can move further toward humanitarian values.

In a mature value system, the parents show an effective concern for children's needs without feeling personally depleted. By placing a high value on children, they can firmly establish their identity as parents, hopefully free of concern about rewards or reputation or status.

The parents most secure in their status as individuals are most capable of acting on the belief that the human race's most valuable asset is its children. Without jeopardizing their own integrity, parents can accept the idea that children are the future and that it is their foundation years that set the stage for later life.

Transmission of Values

Morality defines values and the behavior appropriate in a particular situation; it guides the individual in governing his actions. It is much more than a series of prohibitions. The inner controls, in an individual who is growing in a healthy manner, are strengthened and pulled together and take on a guiding and sustaining role in conduct and human relationships. Morality is a basic mechanism that directs a person's life and integrates his personality and allows him to live harmoniously with others despite the population density of our modern society.

Among the many tasks that a parent helps his child to accomplish on the way to adulthood, two relate particularly to values: development of internal controls and construction of an individual moral philosophy. In helping his child, the parent works with the same problems within himself—successfully or unsuccessfully. The parent may thus strengthen or weaken his inner integrity and functioning. The child has to learn to live with heightened impulses and to find a balance between desire and restraint. He should be helped to build a system of values that will serve as a guide to conduct in his own particular circumstances, a working system that will be his own and not just a rigid imitation of what he has been taught to believe. In this process of "moral" development the child develops character.

A functioning society needs a common core of accepted values to give it cohesion and minimal stability. In the United States this core of values seems to be losing its powers in the face of rising crime rates, incivility, shoddy work, and lack of personal discipline. Whether the educational system should or should not contribute to the family's role in this is a point of disagreement among differing philosophies of education. Some educators have advocated that education commit itself to such a program through the use of textbooks and other readings that illustrate the moral lessons that all children should learn. They are aware that there would be strenuous objections to indoctrinating all students with middle-class values but believe these to be sound and wholesome values. They feel that any society that does not have enough self-confidence in its fundamental values to instruct the young in them or enough common sense to do so is courting disaster.

The values at issue are: honesty and truthfulness; trustworthiness; work well done; kindness and compassion; the courage to admit mistakes; racial tolerance; respect for law; non-violence in pursuit of one's goals; respect for democratic rights. Surely these should all be part of an adult's value system and should be transmitted to the children by action as well as word.

EXPLORATION OF VALUES

There are three significant areas in which young people carry out their exploration of values and try out their controls and search for the type of person they want to be—religion, social idealism, and sex. Parents cannot help being affected by these activities. They are forced, to some degree, to reassess their own religious attitudes, values, and standards during both the spoken and non-verbal communication with questioning, growing children.

Religion.   The adolescent, as part of his movement toward independence, examines the religious attitudes, values, and standards given him by his family and his culture. He may discard certain of the religious beliefs of childhood as he searches for his own set of values and his own identity. He compares his religious beliefs with those of his peer-group members. (This process usually results in some change, but it can be anything from abandonment to renewed intensity.)

Often his rebellion is against what he *thought* was taught him, not what he actually was taught. Sometimes he rebels because what he has been taught is different from what is practiced. In general, he is basically rejecting not a mature religious belief, but his own childhood conceptions. Many years may pass before he realizes that his rebellion was not so much against parents, church, or culture as against his own immaturity. However, few things are so upsetting to parents as an adolescent, struggling with emancipation, who attacks their treasured value system. It may shake the parents' security and cause the child to be experienced as obnoxious.[2]

In order to carry out this process of testing and questioning, adolescents first need to be exposed to some structure or order of religion or humanistic values. There are parents who are not religious but still transmit such values. Some parents feel that they are doing the child a favor in not presenting specific religious beliefs, or by exposing him to a large number in the hope that he will pick out the ones he wants to keep as he matures. It may well be that permissiveness and obscurity in religion give the adolescent nothing to rebel against or depend on. It is as if he wanted something crisp and exciting to chew on and all he had was vanilla pudding. In a society that permits many different kinds of religious values and beliefs, the adolescent's religious conflicts may not be as easy to resolve as in a society with a more structured set of values and points of view. Since religious tolerance is a desirable value in society, the parents' understanding of this problem is most important.

Particularly difficult for parents to weather with a sense of perspective is the adolescent stage of atheism ("agnosticism" would probably be a better word for it). Usually this involves the young person's relationship to his father and to the being he calls God. In the small child the religious experience is closely bound up with his experiences with his parents. God is thought of in essentially the same way as the father. The father or some other figure important to the child might be his picture of God.

If development proceeds normally, the young person learns to separate the two; parents are seen as less divine and more human, and God becomes less identified with the father. This separation is one of the tasks of adolescence; in the process the adolescent may reject God or father or both. This is a normal phase and usually transient. Even when it is of relatively short duration it is trying and perplexing to the parents. As the child works through his rebellion and gains a firmer idea of his own identity, he arrives at a new relationship with both God and father. He is then free to use religious beliefs in an appropriate and constructive manner.

Social idealism. During the inner struggles of adolescence social concerns are often an important part of the young person's life. The reasons for human existence are heatedly debated, and the desire to do something to improve the world is conspicuously present. Sometimes this is blended with religious aspirations. As one would suspect, this religious-social idealism springs partly from the fact that the young person is going through a very turbulent time, and he projects his inner turmoil onto the world outside. "Everything is in chaos," he thinks. "I've got to do something about straightening it out!" He does not realize that a great deal of the chaos is inside him.

Upheaval in the outer world makes the inner conflict more intense. In a time of great social change the work of adolescence becomes much more difficult. A stable environment helps greatly to provide an anchor, and even more important than a stable physical environment is a stable emotional one. In a recent study carried out with a hundred college students, a number of them spoke of conflicts related to social and religious issues, and hypocrisy was one of the things that caused them pain and confusion. They were especially distressed by the efforts of "religious" adults to bend religious teachings in order to justify their particular hates, prejudices, or bigotry. The students stated that they would have been less shaken if the adult world had acknowledged religious precepts as ideal and at the same time admitted their inability to attain that ideal in all their actions. Twisting and distorting the structure of religious idealism left them with no fixed point by which to orient their values or their conduct.[3]

In the young person's search for inner harmony nothing is more helpful than an adult example of mutual understanding, co-operative living, and devotion to the principle of equality for all human beings. Respect for personality, regard for the rights and feelings of others, and commitment to the common good are ethical values that the young person can hold on to and see as functional and valuable while he sorts out his specific beliefs and modes of action. Again, the child unknowingly gives the parent the opportunity for reassessment and personal growth.

The opposite of social idealism involves the phenomenon of prejudice and its transmission from parents to children. The best definition of prejudice is probably the popular, informal one: "Prejudice is being down on something you're not up on." It is similar in meaning to a more formal definition by Thomas Aquinas: "Thinking ill of others without sufficient warrant." The variables involved in prejudice are hostility, ignorance, and erroneous judgment.

Parental involvement in children's prejudices occurs in a variety of ways. In the most direct form the negative feelings and biases about certain individuals and groups are expressed by precept and example in the presence of children. Both the personality structure of the parents and the atmosphere in the home contribute to the open-mindedness or prejudice of the children. A study of prejudice in children at the sixth-grade level revealed a connection between prejudice and child-training in the home. The prejudiced children had mothers who believed in firm punishment, including whipping, who believed that the child should not talk back, and so on. They were much more authoritarian on the whole. The mothers with the non-prejudiced children were more open, democratic, and benevolent in their attitudes.

What the child absorbs in the home is blended with what he observes and experiences in the outside world. As parents observe the child's actions and listen to his ideas, be they negative or positive, they are forced to re-examine their own views and actions in the light of the value system they espouse.

Sexuality. Genital sex—the biological functions of male and female—is only a small part of complete sexuality, which is a person's whole identification as a man or a woman.

Eric H. Erikson, the eminent psychologist, analyzing the developmental tasks of adolescence and early adulthood, puts the development of individual identity before the development of the capacity for intimacy. By this he means that a person must know who he is before he can share himself closely with another person. Unless his own identity is well established, intimacy may bring psychological fragmentation.

Society's intense preoccupation with genital sexuality has created both moral and identity problems for the developing person and confusion within the parents as to their responsibilities. Free sexual expression appears to be encouraged on all sides, with the implication that sexuality is the only form of identity that matters. A particularly dangerous aspect of this is the exploitation of sex to sell merchandise. Those segments of society which attempt to control sexuality seem inadvertently to call undue attention to it. Many researchers have pointed out that when a group insists on suppressing the sex instinct in everything, it betrays the fact that it really sees that instinct everywhere it looks.

Parents are often puzzled by the fact that young people link social consciousness and sexuality. Nothing is more evident in the adolescent than a heightened sense of the erotic. Simultaneously he experiences a widening and deepening of the ocean of goodwill. The different types of love sustain, feed, and strengthen one another; the feeling of love that permeates his life and helps him relate to the opposite sex is closely akin to his love for God and for other human beings. When he carries a sign saying "Make love, not war," his statement may appear depraved to many adults, but it is not. His involvement in social reforms and social action is not just a sublimation of his sexual drives but an expression of those same powerful forces in a different area of his life. Most adults, on the other hand, draw a sharp dividing line between genital sexuality and social consciousness. This is where the parents can learn from an adolescent child. The fragmentation of the various approaches to love has made the adult miss the wider dimension of personal love, the totality with which love can engage the whole of one's personality.

ROLE MODELS AND SEX EDUCATION

In the past the roles of mother and father in the family were clearly defined and quite separate. Few expected the father to help with the housework or the mother to earn a substantial portion of the family income; if either of these conditions occurred, it was in response to an emergency or implied that "something was wrong" with the family and its members. Today, when there is much more freedom to share roles, children still need to learn from family life that men and women do have different, complementary roles, need each other, and need to take care of each other.

The child's understanding of sex roles as he learns them from his parents is highly influential in how he assimilates what he learns about sex. The average child knows a good deal about sex even if he does not receive formal sex education in home or school. ("Sex education is nothing new," one teacher said to another. "We had it when I was going to school, but in those days we called it recess.") Though children today are less likely to suffer a sense of guilt and shame, they can still be disturbed and inhibited about sex. It is important for the parents to have a warm and loving relationship and to show the child that love and sex belong together. Sex instruction, whenever given, should be given in such a way that the child can recognize its relationship to other experiences and not think of sex as an activity separated from or even opposed to other aspects of living.

In many communities parents are taking part in discussions on whether there should be sex education in the schools and, if so, what types of sex education are most suitable for children of various ages. There is a wide variation of opinion even among experts on this subject. A complicating factor is that even if each child receives the same information in class, the parents' unspoken feelings will be conveyed to their children, and so the children will have very different emotional reactions to what they are learning. Many parents are embarrassed about sex, frustrated over their own less-than-perfect sexual adjustment, and disturbed over the new openness about sex (quite apart from any change in moral standards). Here again is an opportunity for parents to work out, through their children, solutions to a common problem.

Most parents know that they should answer children's questions directly, give the information requested but not confuse the child with material for which he is not ready, and discuss whatever topics come up with full attention and without embarrassment. Perhaps the most important part of sex education is not related to sex and reproduction *per se* but to the development of social values, self-respect, and respect for others. Without this over-all personal development, free and uninhibited sex can easily be used in the service of unhealthy goals: proof of power, exploitation of others, self-aggrandizement, and so forth. Good sex education means the achievement by each individual of sexual selfhood and the development of his capacity to use his sexuality creatively and responsibly in all of his human relationships. Sex education is not just an academic subject but a psychodynamic process continuing for a lifetime.

Helping the Child to Develop Values

Although the child must ultimately decide on his own set of moral values, the development of conscience does not occur in a vacuum. It comes about because the child identifies with significant persons in his life and follows their values. As he sees that these same values are good for him, he absorbs them and makes them his own. In an unstable environment, in situations such as moving from one foster home to another, parents' divorce and remarriage, inconsistent discipline, serious physical maltreatment, or lack of love and emotional care—it is extremely difficult, if not impossible, for the child to establish a stable relationship or to accept the parents' values.

Everyone responds to new experiences. The child, because his personality is still in the process of being molded, responds more strongly than an older person, and stimuli have a more definite effect on him. The parent's new responsibilities also make him more sensitive to the new stimuli. Every stimulus from the family environment is a message that both the child and parent have to interpret. If it is direct and clear, they receive it without confusion and act on it; but if they receive a message at one level that is contradicted on another, they develop inconsistent and conflicting images that cause great confusion in the family.

The person who says one thing and does another affects others in the family. The classic example is the mother who filches extra spending money for her son from her responsible, hard-working husband, and the boy knows it. He sees one important person in his life stealing and the other being honest. As an adult, he spends his life struggling between indulging himself illegally (as his mother did) and being a responsible worker and family man (like his father). The confusion in values that his parents created causes guilt and ambiguity that last into adulthood.

What the child learns from the entire society he sees around him can cause even greater confusion. Society has, for better or worse, adopted "middle-class" goals that portray the American dream of unlimited opportunity, material success, education, and status. At the same time, society denies children from the lower socio-economic levels the chance to achieve those goals. Middle-class children learn the social ideals of "success," learn also from their parents that they can and should achieve such "success," and are helped by their family to achieve it. In their case the values are consistent.

Youngsters from depressed groups find that what society teaches them is not applicable to their lives. They have little direct contact with "successful" persons, often lack an adequate family life, and are unsure about how to find legitimate ways of being recognized. Often their parents are very bitter and hostile toward the middle-class world, which holds out ideals that they cannot achieve, and the children reflect this bitterness and hostility. In addition to coping with the conflict in values, they have to seek methods of satisfaction, and since society will not give them the status they seek, they have to look outside it. They find groups with values they can achieve, values that are often detrimental to a stable society. Status may depend on prowess in fighting, drug-taking, destroying lives or property, or taking by force or stealth what cannot be obtained legitimately.

It is not always the parents' poverty or lack of education that is damaging to their children. It is the contradictions in a society that says, "Everyone should have an education, sufficient income, an opportunity to accomplish as much as he can, and the training that will help him achieve these," and then does not provide what is necessary in order for him to achieve these goals.

The same contradiction occurs when a teen-ager finds it necessary to identify closely not just with family, neighborhood, and city, but with a larger community such as the nation. A clear identification is difficult when a country describes itself as a democracy but practices expediency, favoritism, or ruthlessness with certain groups within the nation and outside it. A youngster may need to identify with his country but sees its values as cruel, hypocritical, and destructive of individual freedom. He may then respond by saying, "If this is my country, I do not belong here. But where do I belong?" Such questioning may be more upsetting than questioning one's own ability to live up to those values.

Not only the disadvantaged have these troubles; youngsters from all socio-economic levels may have difficulty committing themselves to ordinary social values. Sometimes intelligent and privileged young people reject the society that has afforded them its best opportunities and advantages. A study of one such group showed that these youths had all been raised in families in which the father, though often highly successful in his work, was withdrawn from the demands of family life and the mother, in consequence, made unreasonable claims for attention and emotional support. The children hated and mistrusted the father and feared the mother's ability to use them against him. Since they never trusted or identified with either parent, they could not identify with anyone else.[4]

Of course, all protesters do not come from disturbed families. Some social inequities are obvious, and recognizing them can be a sign of healthy family values transmitted by parents. This has been shown by a study of two hundred highly successful college students who were asked what in their background or life experience had kept them on an effective and goal-oriented path.[5] The majority of students identified family as the most important motivational factor in their life, and they often mentioned particular values. Characteristics of their families included firmness, neither overly permissive nor rigid; direction without dictation; rules that made sense; high expectations of all family members; and mutual trust and respect. The parents had their precepts and lived up to them. Consistency of precept and practice was noted with appreciation by the students.

At times all of these students rebelled against the demands and value systems of their families, but this rebellion was generally verbal and rarely took the form of acting-out or destructive behavior such as experimenting with drugs or quitting school. Their home seemed to save them from severe identity crises, for they usually had a strong feeling of who they were and where they were going. Not all of the students were close to their parents, but they were able to communicate and share their concerns, fears, and hopes. The parents were available when needed. For many of the students, the time their parents gave them seemed to outweigh in importance everything else they received.

Tied closely to the giving of time was the feeling communicated by the parents: "You are somebody." Thus they did not want to disappoint their parents; but, more important, their self-esteem and sense of worth seemed to push them toward fulfillment of their capabilities. The families covered a considerable socio-economic range, from very modest earnings to great affluence, but values were similar in spite of differences in material resources.

In the young person's search for acceptable values, he needs to live in a state of creative tension regarding morality. He must continually balance and weigh his actions in terms of how abstract principles can be put into action within the context of his group's values and his own personal values. Morality can never be completely an individual matter, because of its necessary relationship to the group as well, and the individual's behavior is integrated by the moral commitments to himself and to his society according to a whole range of social values.

These various demands upon a person's values always cause conflict and tension, calling for compromise and adjustment. Parents should temper their legitimate concern over value transmission with the realization that a child must test the values he has learned. He must see if they really work; he must incorporate them into the pattern of what he *wants* to do, rather than what he *must* do.

THE ROLE OF THE PARENT

In the area of values, it is necessary for the parents to establish a working set of values for themselves—not "super-modern" or "loose-minded" but open-minded. Parents need not accept value-lessness as a way of life. They have a right and duty to advocate particular values and expectations; they have the right to attempt to pass these values on to their children. However, they must respect the child's right to go through a phase of living in which he contradicts parental or societal values or establishes different values. This is not a negative reflection upon the parents. It is in the nature of the child-parent relationship and at times may reflect positively upon the parents' rearing of the child.

Communication, which is a positive value, can go a long way, but there may come a point when communication has to come to an end and action take place. An example is the college girl who brings her boyfriend home and demands that they be allowed to sleep together in her bedroom. It is within the daughter's values not to be hypocritical, and she is being true to herself in taking this position. It is not within the mother's values to condone this behavior, and she finally has to say (in order to be true to herself), "You may sleep with your boyfriend if you wish, but not in my house." Holding the line can be an act of love.

Parents should feel free to offer love, as well as direction and education. Love is a vehicle for transmission of values. Children will use value systems to pressure parents, to rebel, to relate to peer groups. It is essential for parents to uphold their own values in order to preserve their integrity. Parents must also re-examine their own values, because throughout life the conscience undergoes modification in the same spiral-like fashion as emotional development. Commitment is essential to a full life. But "commitment" is essentially a neutral term. One has to ask, "Commitment to what?"

| | DISCIPLINE—
four | SELF AND IMPOSED

CHANGING PARENTAL ATTITUDES

In the window of a Washington toy shop there is a large poster telling of the changing "Advice to Parents" over the past sixty years. Though perhaps not completely accurate, it reflects some of the confusion felt by parents over discipline.

> 1910 — Spank them
> 1920 — Deprive them
> 1930 — Ignore them
> 1940 — Reason with them
> 1950 — Love them
> 1960 — Spank them lovingly
> 1970 — THE HELL WITH THEM!

The anger in the 1970 attitude may be a cover-up or a prelude to the despair and depression parents feel when they have lost confidence in their ability to succeed as parents. Another example of parental attitudes exposed through humor is the founding in 1972 of an organization called Parents Lib. Its battle cry is that parents be totally dedicated and committed to the absolute severance of umbilical cords, past, present, and future.

Life was simpler several generations ago, and most rights and responsibilities were more clearly defined for both parents and children. There was no question as to who was the authority—it was the parents, usually the father. Family life was simpler and clearly structured, job and career possibilities were limited, and parents were seldom called upon for direction and guidance. Misbehavior could be dismissed by ascribing it to natural wickedness or the inheritance of bad traits, and every family had its "black sheep" who served as a scapegoat. Little thought was given to the relationship between how a child was treated and how he behaved.

The predominant impetus in the socialization of the young was in the direction of training for unquestioning obedience and respect for authority with corporal punishment given not only regularly but sometimes as a sacred duty. Chastisement was designed to humble children and to break their wills. The prevailing philosophy was that a child must be motivated by threats and punishments to learn to behave himself, to acquire knowledge, and to become a useful member of society.

During the twentieth century, with the increase in knowledge about how a person grows and learns, there has been a change toward warmth, affection, and respect for the rights of children. Parents have an added burden; they must be aware that their words and actions and what they are themselves affect the children and the way the children act; and they must be wary of acting out their own difficulties in administering discipline. Discipline has grown to include knowledge of how children grow and develop; the application of this knowledge; patience, tolerance, and fairness; flexibility, respect, and love.

THE PRACTICE OF DISCIPLINE

The word "discipline" has many uses and many definitions: a method of training, a system of rules, a state of orderliness gained through self-control, punishment by someone in authority. Many people have accepted the last definition as the only correct one. "Discipline" has meant enforcing one's will upon a child by harshness and strictness, with the goal of obedience being foremost. The child was made to behave, and that was that.

Now it is recognized that discipline (which comes from a Latin word referring to learning) involves more than this. It is the process of organizing one's impulses for the attainment of self-control and self-direction. It is based on the parent's understanding of his children and knowing their strengths and weaknesses. Since particular skills must also be learned, "discipline" is a twofold concept: the guidance and control the parent exerts on the child, and the inner control and self-guidance of the parent.

Without any question, discipline is a natural and necessary tool for the parents of today who hope to raise happy, successful, and mature individuals. It is essential for growth and security. No family, community, nation, or any other human society can run smoothly without a system of regulations and some means of enforcing them. No person can participate in any group without subjecting himself to control.[1] Children, especially, need to know that there are people in their lives who will interpret limits clearly and reasonably. Since children are really the disciples of their parents, they will learn from their parents' leadership and guidance, from the roles their parents play, and from the essential personalities of the parents. Disciple and discipline are connected; to teach a disciple truly is to teach and act out discipline, for both teacher and student or parent and child.

The best discipline is that which leads the child from outer controls to self-control, to a desire for consideration of others, and to appropriate ways of conforming to the outer world. It is necessary for adults to safeguard children from the consequences of those acts which are more than they can handle. In situations involving physical danger, in social situations when they cannot yet judge for themselves, in places where their uncontrolled aggressive feelings are aroused, children need to know that their parents understand and can and will set limits and control their behavior. The range of necessary restrictions in early childhood is so extensive that it is advisable to cut out every possible unimportant and artificial rule. Parents generally manage their children in the earliest years by example, positive suggestion, distraction, leading, appealing to their desire to be grown up, and by physical removal. As children begin to sense what parents do and do not want, parents rely more on verbal requests, realizing that they have to be reasonably consistent and must feel, speak, and act as if they expected to be obeyed. Parental expectation in the area of discipline is a very important force. The parent confident in his own authority expects appropriate self-control on the part of the child and has fewer disciplinary problems. All other things being equal, the person the child loves and admires is the one the child obeys. It is the child's pleasure to give pleasure to those he loves and by whom he feels loved. However, there is one factor that affects this principle—the factor of time spent with the child. The person who spends the most time with the child, the one on whose presence the child can depend even if not loved and admired, becomes the one who is obeyed and copied. Identification with the constantly present aggressor is commonly observed in young children.

The child will not find the limits easy to accept. He learns quickly enough to distinguish between which act is approved and which is disapproved; the problem is making him *want* to do the right thing, rather than feel he has to follow a rule because of the consequences if he does not. The child learns most easily when, because of his good relationship with his parents, he wants to please them. The relationship of trust and affection also keeps the parents sure enough of their child's love so that they can act with objectivity. They do not need to fear that every whim is an expression of the child's need, or feel frightened and guilty when they assert authority or refuse to gratify every wish.

Older children need parents who will stand behind them firmly with advice and guidance but who are mature enough themselves to give up authority gradually as the need for it passes. Little by little, control from without gives way to control from within, and, helped by the parents, the child accepts increasing responsibility for his own behavior. In this process the parents learn to accept increasing responsibility for their own behavior and inadvertently become a better model for their disciples.

Whenever the cause and effect are clearly enough related, the parents can help the child see that what happens to him comes about through his own earlier behavior. This is sound learning technique, far more effective than controlling behavior only on the basis of threats, promises, or orders, which can never create the internal orderliness gained from self-control or build a technique for coping with new situations.

In any discussion of children, it is important to keep in mind the fact that there are differences among children. Some of the differences can be recognized at birth. Not only are there innate psychological differences among infants, but they may be of such a kind and degree as to evoke very different responses from the behavioral repertoire of a given father or mother.[2] These innate differences (temperament) evoke negative or positive responses from parents. Some children tend to be passive and submit readily. Others display provocative behavior, which is often an attempt at mastery, a way of actively doing instead of being passively submissive. The recognition of individual differences in children and of different responses from the children to the same parental activity relieves parental guilt and anxiety and facilitates acceptance of the child as a unique individual.

Cold, rejecting parents may not seem to have behavior problems with their children, but immediate peace is not the goal. Long-term self-discipline is. If the child has no admired adult whose wishes he can use, he may not succeed in "internalizing" his controls. Other parents expect not to be able to control their children (perhaps they were allowed to get away with misbehavior when they were young) and become frightened and confused when forced to work through their own unsuccessfully handled problem in this area. They cannot act as leaders and must fight at the child's level rather than guide him. If mother and father cannot work with each other to apply the same rules and maintain a constant attitude, the child can never learn what is expected of him. He does not learn self-control, but he does learn the techniques for manipulating adults. If the rules are changeable, he reasons, so are the adults. His job, rather than learning how to behave within the system of rules, becomes learning how to get around his parents.

In many parents' thinking "permissiveness" and "license" have become confused. Recommendations for more freedom and self-determination for the children have been taken to mean that little or nothing should be done to control them. Parents who are afraid of their children or unwilling or unable to take a definite stand on anything also misunderstand these terms.

Permissiveness involves accepting the childishness of children.[3] It allows them their own feelings, fantasies, thoughts, and dreams; it brings confidence and an increasing capacity to express feelings and thoughts. Permissiveness is necessary if the child is to develop his full potential without cramping or constriction.

The avoidance of necessary responsibility, of setting sensible limits, of taking a stand on important issues is overpermissiveness, which leads to lack of control, rudeness, aggressiveness, all the negative qualities that are so obvious in the child who has received too little parental guidance.

The belief that there should be complete freedom, or license, is a serious mistake, for children do not have either the background, knowledge, wisdom, or judgment to handle such freedom. Parents must establish limits in order to protect the child in situations that are beyond his competence and to enable the child to recognize the demands being placed on him. Otherwise the child cannot learn to control himself. Learning becomes almost impossible, and the child spends much of his time testing the situation to see if any rules exist.

Overpermissiveness developed as a rebound from the idea of strict control, rigid schedules, and authoritarian discipline. As often happens, the swing was exaggerated, and the children suffered from too little control. Overpermissiveness may sometimes occur in the case of parents who have been strictly brought up, never daring to act, speak, or think aggressively. They use their own children to express the unreasoned spontaneity and aggressiveness they were denied, and their own psychological necessity blinds them to the fact that the child's behavior is offensive to others and disturbing to the child.

Parents can make definite demands firmly, since conditions are most readily accepted when it is clear that parents mean what they say. But firmness should not slip over into domination—trying to force one's will on the child. Firmness without domination requires practice in mutual respect. Parents must respect the child's right to decide what he intends to do, and respect also their own competence by refusing to be placed at the mercy of an unruly and capricious child. They must temper their firmness with enough flexibility to make exceptions when necessary, and enough humanity to admit when they are wrong. The parents' own personalities and the forms of family interaction have a great deal to do with how the balance between permissiveness and firmness is worked out in everyday life. Some parents, without guilt or submissiveness, can be remarkably uncontrolling without spoiling; others, without harshness or irritability, can be quite

72

strict and still not cramp the development of their children. There is no one way for all parents. Whichever way is used by a parent should be his way and consistently so.

Punishment

Frequent misbehavior or failure of a child to live up to what is expected by the school, family, or parents is particularly painful for the parents because of their sense of failure at what is their most important job. They become angry and upset at themselves as well as at the child. Often they tend to lash out blindly without doing what is first necessary—understanding the problem before ╳ trying to solve it. It is more important to look into the causes of disobedience than to put faith in control by punishment alone. Are the demands on the child too great? Do they fit the child, his particular personality, his age, temperament, and sex? Are they suited to the child's needs and abilities at his particular stage of development? Is discipline clear? Is the child being forced into compliance by bullying, bribing, yelling, and hitting? What are the child's feelings about his parents and those who have authority over him? [4]

Parents are increasingly aware that it is unwise to make children ashamed of their feelings. They must, of course, help the children control their acts by setting limits, but they should also take the child's feelings into account. This requires an individualized approach, for every child has different feelings and different reactions. The old adage of "spare the rod and spoil the child" belongs to the days when the only meaning of discipline

73

was punishment and the only method of training was by force and pain. Discipline does bring some conflict, but it is (or should be) a conflict aimed not just at ensuring the desired behavior but at training in self-control.

Good discipline is a positive force directed toward what the child is allowed to do rather than what he is forbidden to do. It is based mainly on mutual love and respect. In childhood it has to be reinforced with teaching, firmness, and reminder. Punishment is only one form of reminder—a particularly vigorous one for those situations which warrant it.

Punishment is no longer seen as the only way to make children behave. To be sure, there will always be times when behavior calls for correction, but the most effective kind of punishment is that which follows logically from the action. It is not a "getting even" or revenge but a mode of teaching. The act should bring its own consequences whenever possible. This cannot always happen, of course. Sometimes the act is far too dangerous, and sometimes it has short-term gains that would reinforce the child's tendency to perform it.

The child who misbehaves frequently knows he should be corrected, and really he wants to be. Often he prefers physical discomfort or a specific penalty that he can count on in advance, so that he can weigh the pleasure of doing what he wants against the punishment he knows will follow. This helps him to see the world as consistent and reliable and is useful when he is young, but ultimately it is a less-than-successful short-cut. It seems easier than the long process of learning to be responsible for doing what he knows is right. No quick substitute has yet been found, however, for the slow development of self-direction and self-discipline.

What the parents do is not nearly so important as *how* they do it. The child's interpretation of how his parents do anything is largely a product of how he feels about them. The child does not become obedient (though he may conform) because of the strength of a punishment; he becomes obedient in response to his desire for approval and his regret at his parents' disapproval. Parents can assist in the process by tempering the quality of their disapproval—explaining why they disapprove, calmly and plainly and briefly—and by strengthening the positive aspects of discipline whenever possible.

All parents punish children at times, even those who solemnly resolve not to. Even the most patient and tolerant parent can be filled with anger at the culmination of a series of intensely irritating actions by the child. Punishment, then, as frequently expresses impatience and anger as the desire for obedience, and parents may show less control of themselves than they would like their children to have. Parents may make lots of mistakes; if these occur against a background of a reasonable, kind, and loving relationship with the children, and the parents can admit their errors and correct them quickly and without grudges, no irreparable damage will be done. Again, what the parent is, is more important than what the parent does.

It is not, after all, the punishment itself that is important. It is the lesson that the punishment is meant to teach. If a child is secure in the feeling that he is loved and wanted, that his parents care about him and have confidence in him, he will not be upset unduly by an occasional slap or other punishment. This is to him an indication that the situation really was serious, that the parent really meant what he said. If the parent has to punish a great deal, however, it indicates a failure of discipline and an unsatisfactory relationship between parent and child. Constant spanking can induce humiliation, leaving the child resentful or intimidated, the parent chronically angry and guilty. More intense forms of corporal punishment indicate a real disruption of the parent-child relationship and are a sign that professional help is needed.

OBJECT OF DISCIPLINE

Rearing children who will become mature, self-disciplined individuals requires mature, self-disciplined adults. However, parents do have moments when they are impatient, angry, or unfair, when all their emotional maturity evaporates. An occasional outburst is not going to cause a major disturbance in the child's growth or harm a fundamentally good relationship. It is part of the child's learning to live with others.

No parents always respond to their children in an ideal way, and they should not try to hold up that kind of ideal for themselves. Parents are human, and children can accept human actions if they can count on the parents' basic love, understanding, and consistency. A child who feels alone, struggling against criticism and hostility, has little chance to internalize the external controls placed on him; while there is no end to the progress a child can make if he knows that there are adults who will help him, guide him, and allow him to go ahead because they have confidence in him.

Reciprocally, when the child reacts positively in this way, the parents' capacity for self-discipline is strengthened. The desire of the parent for his child to be proud of him, to love and admire him, is as strong an influence on parental behavior as similar needs in the child are on the child's behavior.

If parents understand what is going on in themselves, then they can better understand what to do and how to respond to their children. There is a child in every parent who needs to learn discipline. There is a parent in every parent who needs to be capable of disciplining the child within himself. Respect the child and the parent within yourself as you would respect the child whom you are parenting. Parenting reactivates the concern with the child in you, and this can be used constructively as concern for the child whom you are parenting. Empathy is a critical component in the relationship between parent and child in all areas of growth and development, but it is particularly needed in the teaching and learning of self-discipline.

five

VARIETIES OF
PARENTHOOD EXPERIENCES

When individuals marry and have children they are either oblivious to the dangers of parenthood or under the general impression that for them the joys will predominate and they will be relatively free of the sorrows.

The joys are experienced when a state of harmony exists among such diverse and powerful forces as the biological and emotional needs of children, the responses and expectations of parents, and the requisites and demands of society. The sorrows occur when these forces are antagonistic and efforts to regain harmony are difficult or even futile. It is apparent that the state of harmony is likely to be achieved less often than disharmony. The relative infrequency of harmony may contribute to heightened pleasures experienced during parenthood during those times when there is harmony.

PREPARATION FOR PARENTHOOD

It is natural for prospective parents to have second thoughts about having a child, for this means a change in the *status quo.* There are arguments pro and con, but in almost all instances most couples by the end of nine months feel they want the baby, even though the pregnancy may have started out with neither of them ready. This is not the same as not wanting a child, which is the feeling of parents who blame each other for failure in contraception in connection with unwanted or unexpected pregnancies.

During pregnancy both parents face psychological problems, which they resolve in small or large part. In the first three months many couples wonder what change in the relationship between them will develop with the coming of their child. Both know there will be a change but not what it will mean. In the second three months they begin to wonder what kind of parents they will be. Will they be adequate to their task? How will they compare to their own parents? Will there be fun in taking care of children? They also come to realize there will be some frustrations in raising children. One has to be able to share one's spouse with a helpless child. Can one bear the separation? And, in the last three months especially, there is the fear that everything may not turn out all right.

A significant part of the preparation to be a parent is making the jump from a self-image of a non-parent to that of parent. During a natural pregnancy the internal change of the self-image is a central experience. The adoptive couple must wait until the baby responds to their care before they feel they are parents. Some authorities believe that it takes adoptive parents longer to make this adjustment. There are opposing views on whether or not the process of natural pregnancy is indeed central to the experience of parenthood. Those who hold to a biological view of parenthood, at least in terms of emphasis, feel that the natural parents are the real parents and that the adoptive parents cannot ever fully feel a total sense of parenthood. Others hold that experience and parental behavior and parent-child relationships provide a full sense of parenthood. Since the human infant, in comparison with other animal newborns, is least developed in terms of instinctive responses to care for itself, and most susceptible to learned responses, the mother-infant relationship and, later, the parents who care for and raise a child are infinitely more important to the child than distress experienced at losing the natural mother.

Adoptive Parents

There have been radical changes in the adoption picture in recent years. With the emphasis on the so-called hard-to-place children, and the shortage of healthy white infants (and even healthy non-white infants), the eligibility criteria for adopting parents have changed, and many more placements are being made with couples who already have natural children.

What prospective childless adoptive parents must go through to obtain a baby gives them their own kind of preparation for parenthood. When infertility is the reason a couple have come to the decision to adopt, they will have gone through a number of growth-inducing experiences in facing the fact that they are unable to produce their own children.

The decision has involved changing a basic expectation that each had. A study has shown that children take it for granted that they will be fertile. So do most adults, until they find out differently. To change an image of oneself from a person who is fertile to that of one who is not is a painful process. Before a husband and wife finally accept the fact of infertility they experience the agony of waiting for pregnancies to materialize, the disappointment of not carrying pregnancies through to completion, and feelings of sadness and loss. There is the self-doubt that has to be faced about the function of one's own body. There are repeated frustrations that must be endured with the failure of progressive medical procedures to result in pregnancy. Then there is the strain of having sexual intercourse subject to ovulation times, not as the result of spontaneous feelings between the spouses.

Along with all these goes the feeling of shame or guilt about not being able to become pregnant. Usually this is felt mostly in relation to one's spouse, but one's parents and parents-in-law may also be involved. Such experiences tend to lower one's self-esteem, which is the biggest hazard of the ordeal. The husband or the wife may unrealistically blame either the self or the mate and perceive the infertility as a punishment for past sins.

When all the medical procedures and examinations are futile, still another self-doubt may be raised. Could the fact of non-fertility have a psychological basis? Does one really want children? A physician might raise this question out of his own frustration and despair because his efforts have failed to result in pregnancy or to provide a definite answer on the cause of the infertility. The question is not an idle one. For everyone, natural and adoptive parents alike, must face the ambivalent feelings inherent in becoming a parent.

Non-fertility in a couple tests the strength of their relationship, as well as of each individually. For each and for each other, the experiences of facing themselves as infertile are painful. Regardless of the source, in general men find it harder to assimilate than do women; often women feel quite protective of their husbands while both are undergoing the preliminaries that will result in the wish to adopt a child. Facing the problem produces the strength and readiness for parenthood.

The adoptive couple face a number of experiences and encounter attitudes that are not common to natural parents. Everyone seems to give support to a couple expecting a child, but this does not seem to be forthcoming to a couple seeking to adopt a child. People do not seem to identify as readily with adoptive parents as with natural parents, and they do not transmit a similar enthusiasm for the adoptive experience. Furthermore, once a couple have adopted a child, they find themselves running into subtle, ambivalent attitudes toward the adoptive experience. They often feel that there is a persistent desire to remind them of the fact of adoption, by such casual remarks as: "When will you tell him he's adopted?" "How did you ever find such a good child?" "Sometimes I wish I had an adopted child along with my other children. I'd want to see if I'd raise him any differently." "Don't you ever wonder what her real parents were like?" These leave the adoptive parents with feelings of discrimination and prejudice. The constant emphasis on the difference between them and natural parents may be infuriating, especially since some adoptive parents deny that there is any difference. This reaction is probably a reflection of the continuing need still to deny the fact of infertility, if it is present, an indication of how painful the experience is.

The desire to be an adequate parent is common to almost all parents, but it is often more intense in adoptive parents. This seems to be more true of adoptive mothers than of fathers, though this may apply to all husbands and wives and may not be specific to adoption.

Adoptive mothers sometimes feel they have a responsibility not only to their child but also to the natural mother who has given her baby up to be raised by another woman. Sometimes, too, rescue fantasies persist. An adoptive mother may feel she has to do a better job as a mother, and be better as a parent, than the natural parent could have been; or she may have negative feelings about the biological mother who has, in fact, rejected the child. Such feelings affect the adoptive parent's later explanation of parentage.

An adoptive mother may be distressed to find that after the new baby enters the family her husband does not seem so close to her as he was before. Some of this is natural, since there is not too much any husband can do except enjoy the baby. In turn, when the wife gives so much of herself to the new baby, the husband may feel he is less important to his wife. The appearance of the new baby may also be a constant reminder of his own possible infertility, if the cause of the infertility is unknown.

A major frustration that a man bears when he and his wife are non-fertile is that he is robbed in some way of feeling he can be the equal of his own father. Although he may perform as well as his father in other parts of his life, not having a child denies him a major way of feeling that he is growing in stature and competence. As a way of dealing with this frustration, some men do not become as involved with their adoptive children as they might ordinarily do with their own. They may feel brotherly rather than fatherly toward their adoptive children.

It is surprising to physicians to encounter a number of adoptive mothers who feel their husbands are one more child in the family, and not really of equal status as a parent.

A major task in the raising of adopted children is to help them accept the fact that they have had another set of parents. The problem varies, depending on the age at which children were adopted and the age at which children are told.

If a child is more than two years of age when he is adopted, he will bring with him into the new family a set of images of the previous parenting adults. The fact that these images are present, and that the child will seemingly not give them up, may be upsetting to some adoptive parents, because the evidence of having had other parents interferes with their fantasies that they will be the most important persons in the child's life. Also, at times, it seems to the adoptive parents that they have the child on loan, that they do not have sole responsibility for him or for his future. As a result, parents who adopt children older than two years often do not feel as close to them as to ones that have been adopted in their first year of life. There is no need to feel guilty about such differences in feeling, because these arise from something over which the adoptive couple has no control, the need of the adopted child to keep his images of his natural parents. Actually, as the child grows, he becomes very clear who his father and mother are by reason of their parenting, and he makes a clear distinction between those parents who cared for him and raised him and those who merely birthed him. Anxieties in the parents can be allevi-

85

ated by the recognition that some of the child's difficulties in adaptation are due to moving to a new part of town or to a new community, changes that are difficult for all children.

There is still controversy as to when to tell children they are adopted. For some parents this uncertainty is upsetting, because many feelings in the adoptive parents are often activated by the necessity to tell their children they are adopted. Most adoptive parents, at some time, have the fantasy of not telling their children they are adopted. The reasons for this are natural. Old hurts will be reactivated; it is a reminder of infertility and of the pain that accompanied it.

Opinion seems to differ on whether adopted children face deep distress when they have to come to grips with the fact that their natural mother gave them up. Some psychiatrists think that the adopted child need not be distressed by this loss. Experience has shown that older parentless children—not only spontaneously, but through their adoptive parents' own conviction—feel that they have gained their adoptive parents rather than lost their "real" parents if they never had these and were brought into adoption from foster homes, institutions, or painful natural-parent situations. It is a peculiar fact of the psychology of adopted children that they rarely have it in their minds that their fathers also did not keep them to rear.

Adoptive parents are naturally reluctant to give their children unsettling and painful news, but they must recognize that this must be done as part of parental responsibility, since it has to do with the very identity of their children. Parents tell their children out of affection for them, and also out of respect for themselves and their children, so that there are no secrets that would interfere with the parent-child relationship. On this basis, the thinking, planning, and execution can be a manifestation of their knowledge that they have the strength and character to inform their children, and their children have the strength to receive such information and cope with it.

The timing grows out of parental awareness that the children are ready for it. Compulsive repetition of the fact of adoption over a period of time, and having no connection with life experiences of the child and parents, makes children suspicious that adoption is a stigma and that their adoptive parents do not like them as much as they would have liked their own. As with all important news, children will ask questions about the facts of their adoption a number of times, unless they get the message they should not ask. A most natural time to bring adoption up is when the child asks where babies come from, and he can then be told that he came from the uterus of another woman. At the same time he can be told that his adoptive parents are happy that he was there when they were looking for a child, that he behaved so pleasingly that they got the idea he wanted to go with them. This thought of himself as contributing in the "choosing" process gives the child some sense that he was not a passive victim of abandonment but did something about what seemed a helpless situation. The child should be encouraged to ask questions about his natural parents and himself. Complete honesty between parents and child will add to the richness and dignity of their relationship.

The years between seven and ten are thought by many experienced people to be a good time to inform a child of his adoption and help him adapt to the idea. Other professionals recommend early recognition of the adoption, as soon as the parent is able and ready. There is a right time for the parent as well as for the child, and the best time for both must be worked out and decided on an individual basis rather than by rule of thumb.

As adopted children grow toward adolescence, they will, in their fantasies about their natural parents, generally come to idealize and even idolize them. To many adoptive parents, it may be a blow to have the absent parents thought better of than they themselves, who daily cope with the tasks of raising children. This fantasy, however, is one way the adopted child deals with the lowered self-esteem and the fact of abandonment that he has to face.

Adolescence is a trying time for families with children born into them, and even worse for the adoptive family. At some point in adolescence adopted children will ask again about their natural parents. Their need to have as much information as they can get may seem to be intense. The normal challenging and confrontation of parents by children may take on painful aspects in adoptive families. Children may use the fact of their adoption against their parents, reminding them that they are not really their children and so they do not have to obey. The belittling of parents that usually takes place at some time during adolescence may be much more distressing to adoptive parents.

Though both adoptive parents and adopted children are subject to certain psychological strains that other parents and children do not have, adoptive families weather the strain of adolescence with as much—or as little—competence as natural families.

In late adolescence some children feel the need to search for their natural parents. They may want to travel to their birthplace if they can, in the hope that some clues relating to their origin might be uncovered. Questions about their birth certificate may be brought up. Fantasies about their natural parents may take on romantic and unreal characteristics. All of this is part of the process of clarifying their identity, a necessary growth experience. Being honest, and telling the adolescent where he can get information if it exists, often are enough to satisfy him. All adolescents fantasize about their parents, some even denying that, or at least wondering whether, their parents really are their own. Since the natural parents of an adopted adolescent are not available to him for reality testing, his fantasies may persist longer.

When the adolescent is eighteen years of age he can legally ask to see his birth certificate in many states. Telling him it is available but that he'll have to wait is important, for making the birth certificate available is something the adoptive parents cannot do, and it makes their child take the responsibility for finding out more about himself when he is ready to learn more.

The rearing of adopted children involves tasks shared by every parent and every child. For adoptive parents, it is the acceptance of the different experiences in themselves and of the uniqueness of their parental tasks that gives them the authority and confidence to find satisfaction in their roles. When adoptive parents become grandparents, they may be a bit envious that their adopted children are having an experience denied to them. But the realization that the children raised wish to become satisfactory parents in their own right, and that this is an outcome of good parenting, is a joy of parenthood hard to surpass.

On Being a Step-Parent

In our society the role of step-parent is poorly defined. There is a considerable body of folklore that pictures a step-parent as being a cruel and depriving person who is out to make life miserable for stepchildren. There have been a number of popular novels and television programs that describe the difficulties and pitfalls in the developing relationships between step-parents, natural parents, and the involved children. Despite much public interest, there is very little scientific writing on the subject.

One of the first problems a step-parent may encounter in joining a family is to accept any unhappy results of prior difficulties as if he were the natural parent. However competent, mature, and artful he or she is as a parent, it may not be possible to succeed completely. The reason is that a step-parent has to share his role with the parent who is missing from the original family—in such parental functions as educational planning for the children, financial support, and coordination of vacation plans and holiday visits if the natural parent is living; in setting up ideals, in moral training, and in religious affiliation if the natural parent is dead. The reality of the natural parent's presence, be he or she dead or alive, is important to the stepchildren's development of their own identity but complicates the role of step-parent.

Some students of this subject feel that a step-parent actually fluctuates between being a parent, a step-parent, and a non-parent. One must know what role one is in and when to change, and to do so without resentment or self-pity. If one lives with stepchildren it is easy to see that in the everyday experiences of living one is a parent in terms of discipline, planning family experiences, and setting limits on children's behavior. One is a step-parent when certain activities, visits, and planning have to be shared with the absent natural parent. One is a non-parent when, for certain reasons, one stands back and lets the spouse handle those aspects of the family relationships in which one is not or does not want to be a part.

Some step-parents are so sensitive and aware of the "wicked stepmother" or "cruel stepfather" stereotype in society that they go to extremes not to take a position or attitude with their step-children about anything or minimize their involvement with them. Sometimes, too, step-parents have to carry the burden of their spouses' oversensitivity to the reactions of the children to the step-parent, and of the step-parent to the children. The natural parent may feel guilty about having separated the children from their other parent and will not allow the step-parent any authority, will interfere enough to render the step-parent impotent in some aspects of the parental roles. Or the natural parent may fervently wish the step-parent to be a full-fledged parent and to act as if he or she were the natural parent.

No step-parent can actually take the place of the natural parent in the home, but some step-parents have the fantasy that they can. They may delude themselves by fantasizing that they are a near-perfect parent compared to the natural parent, and the children will therefore like them more. The children will frequently interpret such behavior as the step-parent's banishing their natural parent from the household, and, naturally, resent it. Some step-parents then withdraw and become non-parents.

Sometimes natural parents are fearful that their step-parent spouses may resent the extra burdens of caring for the children and may even feel guilty about imposing on them the tasks of raising children. It is not uncommon in such circumstances that the natural parent in the family may keep more control of the children than is required in order to relieve the step-parent of the extra responsibility, which the children may interpret as rejection of them on the step-parent's part.

Actually one's ability to function as a step-parent is very much dependent on how one feels one is doing in the eyes of one's spouse and the stepchildren. The growth of confidence in one's new role as step-parent is highly influenced by the feedback from the family. Attitudes toward step-parents are shaped by the many complex feelings that accompany the transition from intact to broken to step-parent families. If divorce was accomplished with anger, hostility, and blame, these feelings usually persist and become part of the step-parent's inheritance when he or she becomes a part of the family. Unresolved relationships between natural parents can interfere with the full development of the relationship between step-parent and spouse. The step-parent may feel that there still is a relationship between the natural parents which often cannot be fully shared. The children may be a reminder that one's spouse was previously married and that a significant tie to that old relationship remains. Jealousy may arise, and fears.

The stepchildren themselves, in ways they are not fully aware of, can interfere with the relationship between step-parent and spouse. When one enters into marriage before any children are on the scene, there is time for the couple to develop their marital roles before they have to develop parental roles. When one marries a spouse with children, both roles need to be developed concurrently. This is difficult under the best of circumstances and becomes much more so when a natural parent and children are still struggling with anger, hostility, and blame left over from the previous marriage. Under such circumstances the children are apt to have intensified feelings about their step-parent.

When a natural parent remarries, the children are called upon to share the parent on whom they are most dependent with another adult who also makes emotional demands on their parent. This is experienced by the children as a psychological separation from their parent and is very often an upsetting experience. A child, especially if young, may feel terror that he will be abandoned by the parent he needs so much and consider the step-parent an unwanted intruder. On the other hand, a child may be so hungry for a significant relationship with a new parent that he literally wishes to have him or her all to himself and may resent the time the newlyweds have to have to themselves. Some children are very confused about having two fathers or two mothers; until they sort out in their own minds the new roles this natural parent and step-parent assume, they are irritable, fearful, and angry. The step-parent needs to make clear early in the relationship with his stepchildren that he or she is not there to take the place of the natural parent.

At times children feel guilty about liking a step-parent better than their absent natural parent. This situation frequently arises when the absent natural parent has made attempts to undermine the relationship between the step-parent and the child. In this instance the child is apt to be more damaged than the step-parent. Sometimes nothing can be done to influence the hostile, destructive natural parent to stop trying to make the child a "go-between" of the two families. A child generally handles this dilemma by tuning out the offending parent, and by withdrawing in part from the relationship as he develops a growing awareness of his parent's behavior. The step-parent can best help by not trying to win him and by not comforting him about his upsetness. A child can be told that his parent's failure was as a spouse; the

93

failure as a parent need not be emphasized. The child will find this out for himself later on, if he is not beginning to sense it already.

A step-parent may find that, after a visit to an absent parent, a child may be irritable and angry. Some of the child's anger at his own natural parents may be displaced onto the step-parent, since it may feel safer to the child to do this. The answer for the step-parent is not to take this anger personally, when he obviously is not responsible for it. To react angrily in retaliation may only verify the child's feelings that he was correct in the first place, and this may interfere with his full acceptance of his good feelings about his step-parent.

A more difficult situation for the step-parent is when he or she marries into a family where the natural parent has died. Frequently the dead parent comes to be overidealized by one or more of the children. Moreover, the guilt felt by the family members about the death may interfere with the normal process of having their memories gradually become less intense. To hold on to the memory of the dead parent, some children will make invidious comparisons. The best way to cope with this situation is to be frank about the good points of the deceased but at the same time not agree to the comparison. Avoiding defensiveness is much the best solution. If the step-parent finds he or she cannot help being defensive, it is wise to consider counseling.

In some families a special problem arises between adolescent children and their step-parent. With one's own parents a child experiences the usual barrier between daughters becoming too close sexually to their fathers, sons to their mothers. The incest taboo in our culture is a strong one. Barriers between step-parents and children of the opposite sex are not as strong, however, and the taboo is not as clear cut.

The ordinary intimacy that usually exists among members of a family may at times become highly sexualized in meaning. Fondling, kissing, and hugging take on meaning beyond the usual parent-child interactions. This is more evident when there is a great difference in the ages of the natural parent and the step-parent. The classic example is that of the middle-aged father with adolescent children who marries a woman who is closer in age to some of the children than to her husband. The channeling and control of sexual feelings in any family are part of its contribution to the future healthy sexual lives of its members. When these feelings threaten to get out of bounds, adolescent children need to be able to appeal to their natural parent for help. If they feel this is not possible, they plan to run away and often do. In some families disturbing emotional symptoms appear, such as depression or hysterical complaints. These are cries for help, and the seeking of help is indicated. Consultations with family advisers, physicians, and counselors are available in most communities.

Recognition of the problems inherent in the step-relationship is a basic step in beginning to work them out.

For many step-parents there are great satisfactions in their family relationships. Many stepchildren have warm feelings toward their step-parent and have gained immeasurably in their growth toward maturity and wisdom in ways they never would have without a step-parent.

On Being a Parent Married to a Step-Parent

If possible, the children should have the chance to become acquainted with their step-parent before the marriage. Preparation and sharing allows children to become familiar with the feelings that accompany the introduction of a new family member. These feelings are generally mixtures of delight, apprehension, confusion as to whether they will be liked by the new parent and whether they will like him or her.

An important consideration in a young child's mind is whether he must give up one of his parents if he acquires a new one. He must clarify for himself the difference between a biological parent and a parent who takes care of his daily needs. The need of a child to keep in communication with his biological parent lies in the fact that so much of his basic identity is related to this person, even though this parent does not rear him.

The natural parent who remains with the children must see to it that the other natural parent still remains important to them. If the parent outside the home is disruptive of the new family, ways must be taken to control this, for no family can live long with chaotic division of itself. But every important step in effecting control and the reasons such steps are necessary for their well-being should be communicated to the children.

The children of course will be getting messages from the resident parent about the new spouse and step-parent. They pick up these attitudes not from words but from the non-verbal communication that is present in facial and body expressions and in word tones and inflections. Trust, confidence, love, caring for, and acceptance are what is desired with enough left over for the children. The children are being asked to share the parent with the step-parent and may experience this either as a loss or as an additional source of love. Once children learn that adults have an emotional and social life apart from them but that they too will be taken care of and loved, they experience relief. To recognize and meet the needs of everyone in the family is a parental burden.

FACING CHRONIC DISABILITY IN A CHILD

Illness is an unfortunate but expected experience of parenthood; a child's chronic illness or disability is always a shock. An acute illness brings strain and worry, but recovery is expected. During convalescence progress toward return to health is daily evident. Chronic illness is a continuing story with no happy ending probable.

Whether the illness or disability is recognized in infancy or at a later period, parents go through the same reactions—shock, disbelief, depression, anger, denial. They seek other diagnoses. Advice, when sought, relates to the parents' responsibility to the child, and little aid is offered to the parents to help them face the problems looming ahead. The effect of the child's condition on the parents is often overlooked. The phenomenon of parental mourning for the child who might have been is not uncommon.

There are still people who believe that a child's illness or disability is divine punishment for the sin of a parent. To them, seeking help for the child is defying God. It is the parents as well as the child who must suffer, and frequently parents suffer more than the child.

Parents often question their part in the tragedy. Are they unfit parents? Was it due to genetic or familial deficiency? Was prenatal care inadequate? Is there another specialist who should be seen? Within parents and in society, protection of the young is seen as a basic parental responsibility, and chronic illness is therefore a constant reminder of failure. An acute illness may also bring on self-questioning, but there is dramatic action to be taken and often a sense of achievement in meeting the emergency.

With chronic illness there is no promise of full return to health. To be told that the child must always take a medication, or be limited in activity or learning, is a heavy sentence to parents and can lead to pity for the child and therefore overprotection.

Today there is a general acceptance of eyeglasses and hearing aids for very young children. Yet comments such as "poor child" are still made by family as well as strangers; rarely is this noted as evidence of parental care and planning. Doubtless grandparents and others in their age group who know they soon will need the same aids tend to protect their own feelings. They forget that in their early years children with poor vision and poor hearing were subjected to malicious teasing by their peers. Braces and prostheses are just beginning to be accepted in the same category as eyeglasses and hearing aids, but these evidences of disability are less easy for parents to accept.

Though there has long been a myth about children's cruelty to disabled or ill children, when children are left to their own devices they accept such children at their own level of functioning. They are frank in saying another child cannot hear or run; they ask the child many questions about what it "feels like"; they give him roles in play that admit his limitation. This is real acceptance of the child as he is. It is adults who advise being "sorry for" a handicapped playmate, who wonder if his disability is not in some way catching or whether it will be copied by other children. The overprotective and fearful parent may so often warn and intervene that both the handicapped child and his playmates assume he is truly "different." It is not the children who will bring unhappiness to the child and his parents as much as other adults, however well meaning. Parents have to learn to deal with the negative attitudes of others.

Inherent in parents is a tendency to compare their offspring with those in other families—else "Beautiful Baby" contests would never exist. Even when comparison is less overt, the parents may wonder why their child had to be handicapped or find themselves trying to will away the reality of the handicap. This is understandable and causes problems only when guilt at the thought results in "smother love" rather than "mother love," or when self-doubt is so great that the parents attempt to push the child to heights far above his abilities. Here the damage is doubtless due more to the child's perceiving how disappointed his parents are in him than to the actual pushing. Many a healthy but unlovely little girl or a healthy but short little boy has experienced this devastating revelation. Each parent has a dream of what his child will be, and it takes time to realize that a child is not a dream but a person in his own right. Perhaps this is even harder for the parent of a handicapped child to do.

Most parents adapt to the handicapped child's needs and abilities, make effective plans for them, and have mature, well-balanced adult sons and daughters as a result. The parents of a girl who was paralyzed after poliomyelitis at the age of thirteen were able to accept with no undertone of pity or sentimentality the fact that she was confined to a wheelchair. They gave her a full life as a teen-ager, saw her marry, have children, and run her own household. Their attitude was shared by the girl's siblings, and later by her husband and her own children.

It is not easy to allow growth when infantilization of the child seems, at short range, to be less hard on him, easier for the family, and delays the venture out of the home. Whether the basic problem is post-polio paralysis, spastic paralysis, diabetes, or retardation, the parents must make the decision as to when the child is ready for the next step, literally and figuratively. The tendency to think "not yet" is to be expected, and sometimes this is the right answer. At times the advice given parents suggests that the so-called "age norms" are laws of the Medes and Persians, which must be followed regardless of the child's individual needs and abilities. This attitude causes all parents problems, and for the parents of a handicapped child the problems are even greater.

Professional counsel as to when a child is ready for new experiences is helpful, but many parents do not have access to such counsel. It is also unfortunate that specialists are able to deal with the disease or disability, and many are able to deal with the child directly, but discussions of the parents' role often stir up so much emotion that they are avoided. Bland reassurance is less kind than practical examination of reality, but it is easier on the giver.

If at all possible, every parent of a handicapped child should have some knowledgeable person with whom he can discuss freely his personal doubts, questions, and feelings. A worry or question that is repressed can become swollen beyond its true dimensions. The ability of the mother and father to talk freely with each other is of immeasurable value, especially if neither has a secret sense of guilt or accusation. Even so, an outside counselor would be helpful at times.

There are many voluntary health associations that concentrate on particular handicaps. They offer three valuable aids: association with other parents with similar problems; programs to improve services and understanding of handicapped children in general; and an opportunity to learn of new advances in training, care, and treatment.

Associating with an organized group of parents allows for discussion of fad treatments, which often victimize parents and can mean expenditures that penalize the whole family and jeopardize future care of the disabled child as well as of his siblings. Not all fads are the product of venal persons, but unfortunately some are. Each parent has an understandable doubt if those involved in established medicine are disapproving of a "new" treatment, but if he can talk about this with a group of parents, a clearer picture of the relation of promises to results can be obtained. Faith that any one person, professional or not, has all the answers is too much to ask of an intelligent, conscientious parent eager to help his child. Within a group of parents, with their many resources, there is some safety.

In so many chronic illnesses there are daily small wearing responsibilities. If the treatment is uncomfortable for the child, it is more so for the parent. Times of medication, trips to doctors and clinics, special foods—all are nagging problems that can lead to tension and worry. Some parents feel only they can meet the child's needs and so build a wall around the unit. This has several undesirable possible results: the child has too few experiences with other caring adults and becomes fearfully dependent on his parents; the parents' world becomes narrower and narrower so they have less to sustain them or to offer the child; and other children in the family may be penalized by never having both parents attending to their activities and thus being, in effect, sacrificed to the handicapped child. For parents to get away for periods is not neglectful of their responsibilities; it is a way of renewing their spirits and an opportunity to see their child's abilities and needs more objectively. It also assures the older handicapped child that he is not a helpless infant who must always be dependent.

A child's limitation may cause parents to concentrate on his negative side. They forget that the child is a person with abilities to be encouraged, that there are things the child can do well. In the end, pity may become the dominant factor. The authors of *Care of the Handicapped Child* make this statement: "Pity, however sincere and well-intentioned, is not good for anyone, straight or deformed, crippled or sound of limb. Because it is bestowed on those considered less fortunate or less able than the one who does the pitying, it makes the object feel inferior. It further weakens the weak, and causes those singled out to receive it for their 'difference' to feel more different. As a parent, you have much better things to give your child than pity." [1] It must be added that pity for the child may in time have a backlash on the parents as self-pity—a reaction that will certainly make the parents' role more difficult.

Every child gains from his parents the inner strength necessary to cope with his world. The handicapped child has a somewhat different world with which to cope, and his parents have a somewhat different task in preparing him. Their problem is to establish reality-measured goals and avoid demanding too much of themselves. They too are human and should allow for normal human feelings and reactions.

PARENTAL REACTIONS TO LOSS

In literature and the mass media, the arrival of a new addition to the family is presented as a time of joy for the parents. In reality, both mother and father may experience a feeling of bereavement, a sense of loss for their previously free and unencumbered state. The mother's reaction following the birth may vary from transient grief to deep-seated depression. Fathers tend to react by denial and acting out. They may be out getting drunk or be involved in activities that prevent their presence at the hospital. Under these circumstances the mother suffers a double loss, loss of her previous state and loss of her husband at a time when she may need him desperately—though her grief may be more from the loss of an idealized image of her husband than from the loss of her pre-mother status. She tends to take her husband's abandonment as a rejection of herself; she is not aware that it may be more a rejection of the father role than of the husband role. Of course it can be both. The activity of the husband is an example of repetition of a historical event in his life. Such repetitions are observed in parents at these times.

The statement "once a parent, always a parent" is more true in attitudes than in reality. Children do grow up and go away; parents are left alone to grieve the loss and move on to the next stage. This is seen from an early age on to the "empty nest syndrome," as described elsewhere. Clinically it has been observed that some mothers report never having felt better than during pregnancy and the first eight to eighteen months of their infants' lives. Then they become anxious or depressed. What is lost here, so early, is control over the infant. Once the infant asserts a personality of his own, a mind of his own, separation begins. This is recognized as the loss of a valued, idealized, needed state.

Death.   During the period of parenthood, as in any other period, the individual may suffer and have to accept deaths. "Bereavement states vary according to the personality of the bereaved, the relationship between the bereaved and the lost loved or valued object, and the values or institutions of the society of which the bereaved is a member." [2]

The loss characteristic of parenthood is perhaps the most cruel and difficult loss for a person to bear: the loss of one's child. This is particularly true in the elderly who, waiting to die, cannot understand why they were not taken instead of the child. The part of them that was being left for immortality has disappeared before they have. Even in the younger parent such loss is severely traumatic. The picture of a psychotic young woman denying the death of her baby by using a substitute object is well known.

Grief is a complex reaction. Normal grief has been described as including "waves of somatic distress lasting from twenty minutes to an hour: a tightness in the throat, frequent crying, sighing, a feeling of emptiness, weakness, and tension, a sense of heaviness, fatigue, lack of appetite, preoccupation with death and the deceased, a feeling of distance from other people and a loss of warmth for other people, including a tendency to respond to them with irritation and anger, handling of other people in a stiff, formal manner and much talking of the deceased." [3]

Crying alone does not constitute working through the loss. It is the content of emotion that matters—the necessity of letting go what no longer exists except in memories. The two opposites, hysteria and stony-faced emotional paralysis, do not constitute healthy grief.

Observations of parents of a dying child show that parental emotions of guilt, grief, and anger are evoked, and expressed in the style of the parent's character. A parent may unremittingly and exclusively dedicate himself to the care of the child; or he may be so overwhelmed with the tragedy of the child's suffering and impending death that he may find it difficult to spend any time with the child.

The death of a child is experienced as unnatural, and parents feel responsibility and guilt. One of man's deepest fears is death before fulfillment. The parent re-experiences this fear as he sees his child's life ending. Parents have a need to find a meaning for the loss of a child. They fear a meaningless death.

Parenthood has been complicated by the inability of modern man to see death as a natural part of life. Although man has a legitimate need to face away from death, excessive camouflage and expulsion of the notion of death lead to a falsification of the essence of man. At the same time the body-count in modern warfare, the killings on highways and in the streets, have made death a daily part of life.

Along with fear of individual death is the uneasy feeling that nothing can be permanent. Yet parents derive from their children a sense of immortality through them they participate in the whole of humanity.

It is difficult for one to ponder death without resources, be they transcendental, inspirational, or existential. If one accepts death as a necessity, rather than as unnatural and an accident, there may be less need to project fear of death outside oneself. This might possibly mute some of the violence of our times. Energies now used in attempting to repress the concept of death would be available for more constructive aspects of living. In other words, death destroys a person but acceptance of the idea of death may save him.

Parents, in coming to terms with their own feelings about death, will not only contribute to their own maturity and understanding of life but help their children by not shutting them out from the realities of death. Increased psychological acceptance of the idea of oncoming death, in the general cultural upbringing but specifically in the interactions of the home, seems called for. Books may help parents in their own growth in this area and, in turn, the growth of their children.[4]

On Being a Single Parent

Divorce, death, and a job requiring long absence from the family are the major causes of separation in a family. In all these experiences there are common factors that affect the well-being of everyone involved.

The most important, perhaps, is the way the parents felt about each other before the separation occurred. Unresolved feelings resulting in loss of love, in anger, and in loss of self-esteem can plague both parents and children if they are not faced and efforts made to resolve them. Here again the parent is faced with changing the image of himself.

The fact that parents are separated by divorce or death does not necessarily mean that they have psychologically separated. Feelings of anger, remorse, guilt, retaliation, sorrow for oneself, and mixtures of both hatred and love can keep an emotional relationship going for long periods after the parents have ceased to live with each other. Feelings of being hurt or of wanting to hurt the other may unconsciously persist. Inability to get the other person out of one's thoughts is also evidence that psychological separation has not yet taken place.

There are two main processes by which psychological separation may be accomplished: by experiencing grief or mourning, and by resolving and facing one's true feelings about one's self. Both of these psychologic experiences take time to master, and both are painful in some degree. Friends, parents, and relatives who can provide true emotional support by their affection and concern are most valuable. They can help, not by preventing one's suffering or interfering with it, but by helping one to handle it. If such persons are not available, an understanding authority figure such as a minister or family physician may be of help. Psychotherapists—psychiatrists, psychologists, social workers—are professionals trained to help in this area.

One's own feelings as a separated parent have to be coped with first because the children, as they go through the experience, will seek help from their parents to resolve their feelings. Despite the fact that one parent can rear children and meet their physical needs, children need two parents for complete psychological growth and development. What this means is that in order for the child to conceptualize himself as a developing person, he must identify himself with two parents, a man and a woman, a father and a mother. If he is exposed to only one parent in his day-to-day living, he will inevitably invent the other in his mind. He will ask many questions, will try in all ways to get some feeling and information about his absent father or mother. If this is not forthcoming, he will in his fantasy create the parent he needs in order to feel good about himself as a person. If parents have not resolved their own feelings about each other, this process in the child will reawaken old feelings, angers, regrets, longings, and whatever else is still there.

Children need some positive information about both parents and about the attitudes of the parents toward them and to each other. For purposes of building their own sense of self and self-respect, they need to know the assets and good qualities of each of their parents as well as those facts that led to ways in which their parents have failed them. They want to know what attracted the parents to each other, what each liked in the other. And although their larger understanding of why the parents separated will come as they become older, children have a need to know why their parents were divorced, why they were incompatible, and, in the case of death, why their parent died.

Children also get the message when one or both parents indicate either by silence or direct statement that they do not care to talk about these subjects. This will make the children seek information elsewhere or adjust to the delay in obtaining it, but they cannot truly drop the subject because it is an unresolved piece of information about themselves and their growing up.

As they grow older children come to recognize and to realize that their parents are not perfect and in their humanity make errors and mistakes. What they find very hard to forgive is when one or both parents derogate and demean each other. They cannot help feeling angry at the parent who does this, for it degrades them also, with a consequent loss of self-esteem. In addition, they tend to become confused about themselves because it becomes harder to separate out what assets and characteristics belong to their parents and what belong to them.

Consider the example of a nine-year-old boy whose divorced father is living away from home. He sees his father fairly regularly and likes many things about him. If he feels that his mother has strong feelings of rejection for his father and feels only negatively about him, he may have difficulty in identifying with his father. As a boy, he needs to like his father in some ways, and even be like him in some ways, but if he feels his mother totally rejects his father, he may begin to feel that his mother cannot really accept him either. Since he likes his mother and is dependent upon her for affection and acceptance he finds himself in conflict about his loyalties.

A major problem for many single parents is loneliness. What this means is that, with the exception of one's children, one feels isolated. The parent who lives with the children and also has a job may have a sense of being trapped, of having no time for himself or herself. In such a situation children frequently go to a day-care center during the day or after school. When their parent returns from work to take them home and take care of them at night, the children often seem more demanding than can be tolerated. Fatigue and sometimes a feeling of helplessness add to the distress.

When this happens, it is time to take a look at one's situation to see what can be modified and what in one's self may be contributing to the crisis. Aside from the harsh reality of having to work and to raise children alone, there may be attitudes that lock one in, such as low self-esteem caused by the hurt of previous experiences. Relating only to one's children may be a protection against intimacy with other adults. Anger and resentment at the other parent, and doing nothing about it, will surely result in further feelings of isolation and deprivation.

Children need to feel that their parents have a life that is apart from them. They do not want to feel that the whole burden of their parents' happiness and unhappiness is on their shoulders. Furthermore, when their parents have a life of their own, the children become clearer sooner about their own separateness. Emotional growth is then much easier and smoother.

Becoming a single parent, after one has been married, brings many changes in social living. Going without a partner to social affairs where friends are all paired off is to many an uneasy experience. One's social and marital difference seems to be constantly on display. Many women feel that social forces tend to push them toward association mainly with adults of their own sex, and their sense of being successful women is sometimes blunted or at least not enhanced.

The need for social contacts is reflected in the growth of groups and services that offer help in this area. Computer-dating services seem to be a permanent part of the scene in many large cities. Single men and women have formed social groups, some initiated by single persons themselves, many as a church-related function. Social and educational opportunities are becoming more generally available. Agencies serving family and children often offer group therapy and educational programs. It is a sign of serious conflict within one's self if one is aware of one's need yet cannot seek out these opportunities. Counseling or therapy would seem indicated.

The phenomenon of single parenthood is effecting some changes in society as the problem becomes more common and as it is more fully accepted.

Some organizations, such as Parents Without Partners and Solo Parents, have been trying to meet this problem. They offer programs dealing with personal needs, family problems, legal and financial difficulties.

Divorced persons may face "second-class-citizenship" experiences, and children of divorced parents may be discriminated against by their peers. Many newly divorced persons feel like failures, and it is important for them to rebuild an adequate sense of self-esteem. Alienated temporarily from the rest of society, they go through a kind of identity crisis all over again. They must learn to come to grips with the idea that admitting their marriage failed does not make them complete failures as human beings.

six | THE MIDDLE YEARS OF PARENTHOOD

CHARACTERISTICS OF THE MIDDLE GENERATION

The age group between youth and senior citizen—from thirty to fifty-five—has been termed "the middle generation." [1] In 1970 it comprised about 20 per cent of the population of the United States. These men and women are faced with a fast-changing world, the confusing mores and attitudes of their children, and the responsibilities of caring for and coping with (parenting) their own elderly parents. While they are handling these responsibilities at home, they are also carrying on their functions in the economic and social life of society. They exhibit dynamic patterns of adulthood and do not remain fixed and unchanging. They continue to grow and develop and adapt to the conditions to which they are exposed. The search for meaning to life appears during this time.

Like the "middle child," they are caught in between, between the problems presented by their children and those presented by their own parents. Some elderly people may no longer be able to take care of themselves and be regressed to a second childhood; others may still be active parents who reserve the right to direct and criticize just as if their offspring were little. Between these two extremes are parents who present a wide variety of problems and dilemmas. The relations between the middle generation and the elderly can stimulate change, as indicated in this pungent sentence: "I never knew I had parents until I became one." Reconciliation and closeness with one's own parents can occur as they are seen from a broader perspective.

This is the time when the natural enmity between generations is clarified. The story is told of a young father who was watching his daughter and his severely authoritarian father playing together. They were obviously delighted with each other. The grandfather treated his granddaughter with open love, affection, and adoration. In amazement the father asked his father, "Why did you never play with me in this way?" To this the older man replied with tenderness in his voice, "Fool, don't you realize that she and I have an enemy in common?"

The experience of parenting allows the adult to appreciate the pains and sorrows his parents endured and enhances his capacity for empathy. Sharing the joy experienced from the youngest generation brings the two older generations closer together.

The simultaneous ambivalence to one's children and one's parents as well as simultaneous responsibility for them has positive effects. It develops the all-important capacity for empathic responses as well as the characteristics of maturity—wisdom, integrity, and the ability to relate on different levels to one's late-adolescent and young-adult children. The pleasures experienced are the pleasures of functioning well, of pulling together the effects of several decades, and these serve as a preparation for grandparenthood.

WHEN CHILDREN MARRY

Though the variations of individual experiences of the middle phase of parenthood may be innumerable, the main characteristic is the parents' involvement in and preoccupation with their children's sexual life.[2] Parents are intent on protecting their children, their daughters more than their sons, against the dangers of premarital sex. The current sexual revolution, touched off by the effectiveness of the birth-control pill and the increasing ease of obtaining legal abortions, has often made the parents feel helpless in the face of their responsibility. Mothers have traditionally been more concerned and preoccupied than fathers, and their worries rarely cease until the child is safely married.

The immediate responsibilities of parenthood are discontinued with a child's marriage. Legally, the child's new mate has become the next of kin. The sudden change, though often a hoped-for relief emotionally, is not easily accepted. Difficulties in giving up parental responsibilities are often satirized in mother-in-law jokes. For women, separation from daughters and sons seems more difficult than for men. This is particularly true if the mother has no other involvements and the father is at the peak of his involvement in his work.

At the time of the marriage of a child the parents have a new developmental task to accomplish.[3] They have to welcome the new in-law, not only into the family but into their hearts, as an object of their love. When a need is being fulfilled, this works out beautifully. There are mothers who accept the new son-in-law wholeheartedly. He may epitomize the son she never had or what her own sons never became. Some fathers adore their son's wife. The newcomer enhances the parents' feelings of self-esteem and pride.

Where parents are overly concerned about the happiness of their child, the problem of ambivalence flares up. They tend to fault the in-law rather than their own child. Here the parents must work to separate themselves from the married child, objectifying their parental relationship, and thus become more objective and less ambivalent toward the in-law.

The Empty Nest

As, one by one the children separate from the home, the nuclear family becomes again just the parents. Some families, of course, never really empty the nest. There may always be a few children at home; there may be grandchildren; the couple may have a late child or become foster parents or adopt children.

A problem that may occur during this period has been labeled "the empty nest syndrome." Some parents evidence attitudes of crisis; others do not. In a recent survey[4] of a group of men and women—primarily Anglo-American in higher blue-collar and clerical occupations—fewer than one in five reported frustrations in the present. Men's frustrations were usually connected with work or money, but they, like the women, were proud of their marriages, their children, and their families. The satisfactions of parenthood continued for both sexes. The prospect of an empty nest seemed not to be a threat. Rather they looked forward with relief to a somewhat less complex life style.

In most cases, the active phase of parenthood does not end with a big bang, a final flash. It fades slowly, like the dimming of the houselights in a theater. Whether that dimming proceeds to total darkness or the curtain lifts on a new and brighter scene depends on how husband and wife have weathered the storms of parenthood, how they have matured, and how they take up their new roles.

The parents are not the same as they were two decades earlier. They have changed physically, for they are approaching or into middle age, and they have changed psychologically, hopefully becoming wiser. Some of their earlier ways of interacting and coping with the outside world are stronger, some have fallen into disuse, and some new ones have developed. Their social roles have changed, for they are no longer a young couple starting a family and career. At the same time society itself has changed. The technological explosion following World War II has been accompanied by a social revolution that has questioned old values, altered patterns of work and family living, and created a culture substantially different from that in which the parents grew up.

Problems of Middle Age

Middle age brings new crises. When the crisis is challenging, something one feels confident about coping with, it can be a means of growth. Other crises may be unmanageable. Business reversals occur; the expected promotion goes to someone else. A close friend or relative dies. Serious illness is diagnosed. It may be that just the process of aging itself begins to be distressing. The telephone book seems to be printed in smaller type each year, theater and airplane seats are not as comfortably wide as they were advertised to be, stairs are getting steeper, a midweek party seems more like an endurance contest than a celebration. The single strand of gray has broadened into streaks. Sagging jowls and double chin seem to have appeared overnight. The body as a whole has less rebound; minor illnesses last longer, and new aches and pains appear with nagging regularity.

Most parents experience these stresses as minor and fleeting inconveniences. They feel in the prime of life and find these years productive and creative. However, the feelings of helplessness and uselessness that can set in are common enough to be recognized as a specific illness—a middle-life depression, also called climacteric depression or involutional melancholia. It affects women more frequently than men, because women are more troubled by the children's leaving home and because the day-to-day care of the children has been the central part of their lives and a heavy emotional investment. At about the same time the woman has to deal with the physical and emotional stresses of menopause.

There are sexual problems to be resolved in this age group. Marriage partners may find it particularly difficult to work these out if their relationship has not been based on mutual trust, understanding, and tolerance. Women are generally more keenly aware of their changing physiology. Men are prone to develop a "now or never" attitude about sex. They may try to bolster up their self-image by means of an extramarital liaison with a younger partner, or prove their sexual prowess with a number of different partners, or experiment with previously untried forms of sexual expression.

In addition to his changing image as a father and as a husband, the man has problems that revolve around his job. What used to be a stimulating test of his ability to succeed becomes a perfunctory routine for warding off failure. The innovative aggressiveness that marked his early years with the firm has given way to a "don't make waves" attitude, a preference for the tried and true methods that worked for him as he climbed the ladder. He is not sure if he can keep on top of what is happening in the organization, or can manage to learn new skills and techniques required by technological changes. He begins to think seriously about the company or union pension plan. How high can he get in the company before his enforced retirement? The higher he can push his earnings before retirement, the better his pension will be. So he tries to sell himself to his superiors but hesitates to take risks that might prove his worth over that of the innovative but less experienced younger men who threaten him.

For both husband and wife, the middle years are often a time of taking inventory, assessing what has been accomplished and what the resources are with which to face the future. This may raise upsetting questions. The man may ask, "If I had done it differently twenty years ago, where would I be now?" The wife remembers that she rejected the proposal of the man who is now president of her husband's company. The husband thinks of his ambition to found his own accounting firm and looks at his position as assistant bookkeeper in one of the company's branch offices.

Major financial demands occur. Husband and wife, worried about building up a reserve for their later years, are faced with paying for a college education, or helping to launch careers, or lending assistance when children get married. Parents who have high aspirations for their children find that their help is especially needed if graduate training is to be completed and a young family started.

The deepest strains are probably psychological. When a child leaves home—for education, to serve in the Armed Forces, to assume a job in a distant place, or to get married—there is an empty place in the family. This is not the first time that parents have felt the wrench of separation. They went through it when the child first began to assert his independence, when he started school, when he reached puberty. Now the loss repeats itself in an irrevocable way, and it rekindles the conflicts that so many parents have about letting go and relinquishing their authority and control. Once more the parents have to spiral around and work out their past conflicts and hopes, this time knowing that the children are physically absent and there is little chance to correct any mistakes made in the past.

A Time for Enjoyment

Every stage of life can be an opportunity to broaden and expand, or a threat causing restriction and retreat. Each stage of life adds new experiences and knowledge—knowledge of one's capabilities and assets, experience in overcoming one's limitations and liabilities, and increasing awareness of what life has to offer. Middle age, particularly, can bring a wealth of contentment and satisfaction. The pressure of youth to challenge, change, and rebel has been tempered by the growing ability to see life as it is, to keep things in proper perspective. The grueling race to find a mate and establish a career has been run; children no longer demand around-the-clock care; and social life is no longer dictated by the caprices of babysitters or the unpredictability of childhood diseases.

There is time now for enjoyment. The parents whose children are grown are free to develop new talents and interests that will not only satisfy their desire for self-expression, but also expand the reservoir of what they have to offer to the society in which they live. They are able to relinquish many of their former responsibilities to the family, and they are ready to assume responsibility for their generation.

seven ⦿ GRANDPARENTHOOD

If the psychology of parenthood was a much neglected field of study, grandparenthood was practically ignored. What few references there were in the literature concerned similarities in grandchildren's gestures and attitudes to that of their grandparents. Some work has now been done in this field. In recent studies grandparenthood has been placed before the last phase of parenthood in the life cycle.[1]

In the grandparents' search for a meaning to life, the grandchildren represent their tie to eternity; a part of them that continues in the stream of life after they have gone. If the grandparent has not established a full life of his own and has an unfulfilled need to be needed, grandchildren are a blessing. Grandchildren have an inexhaustible supply of needs, more than enough to go around for all the adults in their environment. The grandparents offer the advantages of the extended family and take some pressure off the nuclear family of father, mother, children.

In observing the growth and development of their grandchildren, grandparents relive the memories of the early phase of their own parenthood. This is the time when the understanding, empathy, and wisdom that come only with age are valuable assets. It should be noted that some grandparents, in trying to make up for the failures with their own children, become less understanding, less responsible, and too indulgent with the grandchildren. Some who fail their children also fail their grandchildren.

EMOTIONAL CONTENT

It is difficult to generalize about this because several variables are involved. There are differences depending on the personalities of the interacting individuals belonging to the three generations, and on the cultural and socio-economic changes in family structures.[2] The need for parental separation from children and emotional independence also holds true for grandparents.

In the United States, with its sociological peculiarities of mobility, extended families are diminishing. Segregation of the elderly is seen as they become infirm. Here emotional self-reliance is especially important.

Change should be anticipated and accepted. When it is, the wisdom and calmness of age are seen. When it is not, the rigidity and irritability in aging are exposed. Experience has shown that older adults do respond to interest by others and opportunities for change.

Parenthood and grandparenthood are stages for continuous growth and development. A continuing involvement in the stream of life delays the concentration of interest on one's self characteristic of emotional preparation for death.

This involvement with life's activities while furthered by interest in grandchildren should not center on them. Grandchildren too grow up and away from grandparents. That they may have time enough or be kind enough to be loving may be balm for the wounds that age inflicts, but this is not sufficient for adaptation. Even in grandparenthood continuing change involving separation and individuation is the order of the day.

Influence of Grandparents

Of the various influences that play a part in the child's development to maturity, the immediate family is, of course, of primary importance. Grandparents also make a significant contribution. To understand this, it is helpful to think of the family as a dynamic system: new members are introduced; existent members are in a constant state of change within themselves and in relation to one another; members drop out of the system at various times, when they go away to college or get married or move out to live on their own. Sometimes what is termed "dropping out" is better described as a change in the relationship to the system. Death of one of the members is an actual physical dropping out. Between grandparents and grandchildren there is not a one-to-one relationship, but a dynamic interrelationship within a dynamic system.

The influence of grandparents varies greatly from family to

family and from culture to culture. In a general way, it can be said that their influence is exerted in two ways: through direct contact of varying intensity; and through what they represent in the family system. It is possible for grandparents to exert a potent influence even though the child has never personally related to them. In many family systems the memory of someone two generations or more in the past may still be a strong force in the lives of some family members.

Obviously where grandchild and grandparents have direct contact the influence is greatest, and this is so whether the grandparents are part of the same household, or live a considerable physical distance away. The actual degree of physical contact is not the significant factor, but rather the relative position the grandparents occupy in the total family system.

It is important to have an awareness of one's origins, and in the family system grandparents usually represent the most remote living expression of a child's origin. They probably convey a feeling about origins that parents cannot. The fact that the grandchild is the visible and tangible expression of the grandparents' continuance adds another ingredient to the relationship.

Where grandparents live in the same household with their children and grandchildren, confusion and rivalry sometimes develop. A grandparent may become the parent while the actual parent is relegated to the position of the child's older sibling, as it were. The parent is at a disadvantage because his feelings for the children are still ambivalent. The grandparents, on the other hand, may have already exhausted their hostility and other adverse feelings on their own children so that little of these are left for the grandchildren. This is why a grandchild sometimes seems to be the recipient only of the grandparents' indulgence.

In some families the grandfather plays an additional part. At the time a grandson is beginning to weave his "family romance" and in his imagination is engaged in replacing his real father with a more satisfactory figure, the grandfather may present himself as an acceptable substitute. The replacement figure is always endowed with the qualities of the father, so that an analysis of the fantasy leads straight back to the father. The grandfather is therefore peculiarly suited to play this part, because of his resemblance and relationship to the father (in the case of the grandfather on the paternal side). The process is often furthered through the greater tenderness and forebearance that mark, as a rule, the attitude of an older man toward children; many a stern father becomes in later life an indulgent grandfather, partly perhaps because his feeling of responsibility in the rearing of children gets dulled with the philosophy of age. As the child grows older, the association already established becomes strengthened by the increasing resemblance of the father to the memory-picture of the grandfather.

The Value of the Family System

In broad terms, what is required during the maturation process is the movement of a child from total helplessness at birth to relative independence at maturity. The family system provides the child with the opportunity for experiencing, in the interaction of the various members of the system, what lies ahead for him as an individual. Through the grandparent, who is at the distant end of the spectrum, the child can establish his origins. He can see the ascendency of the parents at the same time as the decline and possible loss of the grandparents. Within the family system he has an opportunity to grapple with a wide range of life's experiences, from birth, marriage, and success to death and failure, with all of the accompanying emotions. To this total experience grandparents contribute significantly.

eight

PARENTS
ARE PEOPLE TOO

The current generation of parents has devoted much of its resources to the development of the young. It has been the guardian of the twentieth-century concept that the rearing of healthy children is a creative act. Yet it is often maligned not only by the younger generations but also, in its confusion, by itself.

Emphasis on the importance of parenthood is a culturally conservative force. Every society, from the earliest aborigine on, has structured some form of family life to rear, socialize, and protect the children. Against this force considerable opposition is developing, as seen in the anti-cultural, deeply individualistic movements. From this viewpoint, the individual is more real, more fundamental, than other levels of abstraction, such as the family life style. Communal types of living, it is said, free the individual from direct responsibility for the child.

Values seem to lie at the core of the dispute. It is consistent with wanting to be a parent to believe that it is more creative to rear and shape the personality of a fine, live child than it is to work in an office or even to carve a statue. It is consistent with the role of the parent to believe that when economic necessity does not compel it, even the best day-care center is a poor substitute for a constant one-to-one relationship of an adequate mother to her child within the setting of a nuclear or extended family. It is also consistent that the parent is an individual in his own right in addition to being a parent.

It may be that the two views have the common goal of developing a healthy mature self but differ in approach—one through parenthood and the other through activities removed from parenthood. The experience of parenthood is not essential for the successful growth and development of an individual to maturity. The experience of parenthood, in itself, does not achieve the goal of emotional maturity. The opportunity may not be utilized positively and may even be a deterrent to self-development in some individuals. For such people the alternative life style of the commune may be more suitable. The successful society of the future is likely to be one that is capable of tolerating many life styles without too many abrasive interactions.

The controversy has tended to make parents feel guilty and anxious in their role. This impedes their personal growth during the parental stage of the life cycle and does not contribute to the welfare of the children.

Since the extended family life style, which has been the mainstay of every earlier civilization, has given way to the nuclear family, its functions are increasingly being taken over by schools, churches, and other community resources. Parents should see to it that these extensions are truly responsive to their needs.

The parents' and grandparents' interest in the children brings about changes in the adults. The parents' behavior is dependent upon their past experiences, their reactions to the presence of the child, and their future expectations. They face continuous adaptation to physiological and psychological changes in the child, and an inner push for self-development is a constant force. By continuing to grow through the stage of parenthood and even grandparenthood the individual becomes more adequate as a parent, a grandparent, and even beyond these years if circumstances create separation from one's family, leaving the individual on his own. It is at this time that the hard-earned wisdom and love of humanity beyond the circle of one's family characteristic of maturity serves the person well.

After centuries in which children were considered to be chattel and to have little rights of their own, a swing of the pendulum has taken place. In the twentieth century their rights have been vociferously presented. In the process parents have been designated as the villains. The present state of confusion among parents, their anxiety and guilt about their role, may force a period of thought and reflection and consideration of a change in priorities.

Parents are not only vehicles for the care of their children. They were persons before the child arrived; are persons while they are parents; and will be after the children leave. Their "old-fashioned" values of love and family are worthwhile. The past is not entirely "dumb." Parents should respect their own values and live by them. They were once told to listen to their parents. They are now told to listen to their children. Both directives are valuable. They must, in addition, listen to themselves. If parents do this, things may not turn out as well as desired, but their fulfillment will be solidly based on their own growth and development.

REFERENCE NOTES

FOR FURTHER READING

INDEX

REFERENCE NOTES

one PARENTHOOD, A PERIOD OF PERSONAL DEVELOPMENT

1. James E. Anthony and Therese Benedek (eds.), *Parenthood: Its Psychology and Psychopathology* (New York: Little, Brown, 1970).
2. *Ibid.*
3. Kahlil Gibran, *The Prophet* (New York: Alfred A. Knopf, 1965), p. 17.
4. Material in this section adapted from Alice S. Rossi, "Transitions to Parenthood," *Journal of Marriage and the Family*," 30:1 (1968), pp. 26–39.
5. David Friedman, "Parent Development," *California Medicine*, 86:1 (1957), pp. 25–28.
6. Erik H. Erikson, *Childhood and Society* (New York: W. W. Norton, 1950), pp. 219–224.
7. *Ibid.*

8. Group for the Advancement of Psychiatry, *Normal Adolescence: Its Dynamics and Impact* (New York: Charles Scribner's Sons, 1968).

two EXPECTATION AND DISAPPOINTMENT IN PARENTHOOD

1. Anthony and Benedek, *op. cit.*
2. C. Knight Aldrich, "Expectations: Great and Otherwise," *Wisconsin Medical Journal*, 62:114–118 (1963).

three THE PSYCHOLOGY OF VALUES

1. Erikson, *op. cit.*
2. Peter A. Martin, "Obnoxiousness in Psychiatric Patients and Others," in *The Psychiatric Forum*, ed. Gene L. Usdin (New York: Brunner/Mazel, 1972), Chapter 9, pp. 59–69.
3. James A. Knight, "Religious-Psychological Conflicts of the Adolescent," in *Adolescence, Care and Counseling*, ed. Gene L. Usdin (Philadelphia: Lippincott, 1967), pp. 31–50.
4. Kenneth Keniston, *The Uncommitted Alienated Youth in American Society* (New York: Harcourt, Brace and World, 1967).
5. James A. Knight, "Resisting the Call of the Cave," *Medical Insight*, 2:66–77 (1970).

four DISCIPLINE—SELF AND IMPOSED

1. Karl S. Bernhardt, *Discipline and Child Guidance* (New York: McGraw-Hill, 1964).
2. E. James Lieberman, "The Disturbing Child and Family Therapy," *Clinical Proceedings of the Children's Hospital*, 27:245–249 (1971).
3. Haim G. Ginott, *Between Parent and Child* (New York: Macmillan, 1965), p. 97.

4. Stella Chess, Alexander Thomas, and Herbert Birch, *Your Child Is a Person* (New York: Viking, 1965), p. 87.

five VARIETIES OF PARENTHOOD EXPERIENCES

1. Edith M. Stern and Elsa Castendyck, *Care of the Handicapped Child* (New York: A. A. Wyn, 1950), p. 18.
2. B. Schoenberg et al. (eds.), *Loss and Grief: Psychological Management in Medical Practice* (New York: Columbia University Press, 1970), p. 35.
3. Erich Lindemann, "Symptomatology and Management of Acute Grief," *American Journal of Psychiatry*, 101:141 (1944); see also E. James Lieberman, "War and the Family: The Psychology of Antigrief," *Modern Medicine*, April 19, 1971, pp. 179.
4. Earl A. Grollman, *Talking About Death* (Boston: Beacon Press, 1970); Earl A. Grollman, ed., *Explaining Death to Children* (Boston: Beacon Press, 1967).

six THE MIDDLE YEARS OF PARENTHOOD

1. Rose N. Franzblau, *The Middle Generation* (New York: Holt, Rinehart & Winston, 1971).
2. Anthony and Benedek, *op. cit.*
3. *Ibid.*
4. M. F. Lowenthal and D. Chiribog, "Transition to the Empty Nest," *Archives of General Psychiatry*, 26:8–14 (1972).

seven GRANDPARENTHOOD

1. Anthony and Benedek, *op. cit.*
2. *Ibid.*

FOR FURTHER READING

Abraham, Karl. "Some Remarks on the Role of Grandparents in the Psychology of Neuroses," *Clinical Papers and Essays on Psychoanalysis*, vol. 2, pp. 44–47. New York: Basic Books, 1955.

Anthony, E. James. " 'It Hurts Me More Than It Hurts You'—An Approach to Discipline as a Two-Way Process." In *From Learning for Love to Love of Learning*, edited by Rudolf Ekstein and Rocco L. Motto, pp. 117–131. New York: Brunner/Mazel, 1969.

Barnard, J. *Remarriage, A Study of Marriage.* New York: Dryden Press, 1956.

Baruch, Dorothy W. *New Ways in Discipline.* New York: McGraw-Hill, 1949

Bettelheim, Bruno. "The Problem of Generations." In *Youth: Change and Challenge*, edited by Erik H. Erikson, pp. 64–92. New York: Basic Books, 1961.

Bowlby, John. *Attachment and Loss*, vol. I, chap. 1. New York: Basic Books, 1969.

Bradley, T. *An Exploration of Caseworkers' Perceptions of Adoptive Applicants*, New York: Child Welfare League of America, 1967.

Bruch, Hilde. *Don't Be Afraid of Your Child*. New York: Farrar, Straus & Young, 1952.

Caldwell, Bettye M. "What Is Optimal Learning Environment for the Young Child?," *American Journal of Orthopsychiatry*, 37:8–21, 1968.

Cann, H. M., and Cavallis, L. L. "Effects of Grandparents and Parental Age, Birth Order and Geographic Variation on Sex Ratio, Live-Born and Still-Born Infants," *American Journal of Human Genetics*, 20:381–391, 1968.

Cornwell, Georgia. "Scapegoating," *American Journal of Nursing*, 67:1862–67, 1967.

Curlee, J. "Alcoholism and the Empty Nest," *Bulletin of the Menninger Clinic*, 33:165–171, 1969.

Deykins, E. Y.; Jacobson, S.; Klerman, G.; and Solomon, M. "The Empty Nest: Psychosocial Aspects of Conflict Between Depressed Women and Their Grown Children," *American Journal of Psychiatry*, 122:1422–26, 1966.

Epstein, Nathan B. "Grandparents and Parents of Emotionally Healthy Adolescents." In *Science and Psychoanalysis*, edited by Jules H. Masserman, vol. 3, pp. 181–188. New York: Grune & Stratton, 1960.

The Exceptional Parent. Psychological Education Corp., 264 Beacon Street, Boston, Mass. 02116.

Faegre, M. L.: "The Cruel Stepmother," *Ladies Home Journal*, February 1935, pp. 72–74.

Fast, I., and Cain, C. C. "The Stepparent Role: Potential for Disturbances in Family Functioning," *American Journal of Orthopsychiatry*, 36:485–491, 1966.

Ferenczi, Sandor. "The Grandfather Complex," *Further Contributions to the Theory and Technique of Psychoanalysis*, pp. 323–324. New York: Basic Books, 1952.

Gardner, Richard A. *The Boys' and Girls' Book About Divorce*. New York: Science House, 1970.

———. "The Guilt Reaction of Parents of Children with Severe Physical Disease," *American Journal of Psychiatry*, 126:636–644, 1969.

"Generation in the Middle," *Blue Print for Health*, Chicago: Blue Cross Association, vol. 23, no. 1, 1970.

Giloran, J. L. "Family Happiness," *Royal Society of Health Journal*, 85: 211–217, 1965.

Gruenberg, Sidonie M., ed. *The New Encyclopedia of Child Care and Guidance*. Garden City, N.Y.: Doubleday and Co., 1968.

Hamovitch, Maurice B. *The Parent and the Fatally Ill Child*. Denver, Colo.: City of Hope Medical Center, 1964.

Hobbs, Daniel F. "Parenthood as a Crisis—A Third Study," *Marriage and the Family*, 27:367–372, 1965.

Holt, Hubert, and Winich, Charles. "Some Psychiatric Dynamics in Divorce and Separation," *Mental Hygiene*, 49: 443–452, 1965.

Johnson, G. P. "Delinquent Boys, Their Parents and Grandparents," *Acta Psychiatrica Scandinavica*, 43, 1967, supplement 195.

Jones, Ernest. "The Significance of the Grandfather for the Fate of the

Individual," *Papers on Psychoanalysis*, 4th ed., pp. 519–524. London: Bailliere, 1938; paperback ed., Boston: Beacon Press, 1961.

Kahana, B. "Grandparents from Perspective of Developing Grandchild," *Gerontologist*, 8:31, 1968.

Kalish, R. A. "Of Children and Grandfathers: A Speculative Essay on Dependency," *Gerontologist*, 1967, 65–69.

Kanner, Leo. *In Defense of Mothers*. Springfield, Ill.: Charles C Thomas, 1951.

Keniston, Kenneth. *Young Radicals*. New York: Harcourt, Brace and World, 1968.

Kirk, H. D. *Shared Fate*. New York: Free Press of Glencoe, 1964.

Lidz, Theodore. "The Person," *Marital Choice*, pp. 386–410. New York: Basic Books, 1968.

Lindemann, Erich. "Problems Related to Grandparents." In *Understanding Your Patient*, edited by S. Liebman, pp. 147–158. Philadelphia: Lippincott, 1957.

Longoer, Thomas S. "Broken Homes and Mental Disorder," *Public Health Reports*, 78:921–926, 1963.

Loomis, W. G. "Use of a Foster Grandmother in Psychotherapy of a Preschool Child on a Pediatric Ward," *Clinical Pediatrics*, 6:384–386, 1967.

Malinowski, Bronislaw. "Parenthood the Basis of Social Structure." In *The New Generation: The Intimate Problems of Modern Parents and Children*, edited by V. F. Calverton. New York: Macauley Co., 1930.

Mendelson, R. S., and Gold, J. G. "A Foster Grandchild Program," *Pediatrics*, 41:691, 1968.

Meriam, A. S. *The Stepfather in the Family*. Chicago: University of Chicago Press, 1940.

Meyerowitz, J. H., and Feldman, Harold. "Transition to Parenthood," *Psychiatric Research Reports* (American Psychiatric Association), 20:78–84, 1966.

McDermott, John T., Jr. "Parental Divorce in Early Childhood," *American Journal of Psychiatry*, 124:1424–32, 1968.

Neubauer, Peter R. "One Parent and His Oedipal Development," *Psychoanalytic Study of the Child*, 15:286–309, 1960.

Pedersen, F. A., and Sullivan, E. J. "Relationships Among Geographical Mobility, Parental Attitudes and Emotional Disturbances in Children," *American Journal of Orthopsychiatry*, 34:575–580, 1964.

Rappaport, Ernest A. "A Grandparent Syndrome," *Psychoanalytic Quarterly*, 27: 518–538, 1958.

Rasmussen, Margaret, ed. *Discipline*. Association for Childhood Education International, Bulletin 99, Washington, D. C., 1956.

Robin, A. J. "Motivation for Parenthood," *Journal of Projective Techniques*, 29:406–413, 1966.

Rogers, Peter. "Influence of Losing One's Parent on Being a Parent," *Psychiatric Digest*, 29:29–36, 1968.

Rybak, W. S. "Psycho-social Changes in Personality During Foster Grandparents Program," *Journal of the American Gerontological Society*, 16:956–959, 1968.

Schecter, M. D. "Observations on Adopted Children," *Archives of General Psychiatry*, 3:21–32, 1960.

Schecter, M. D.; Carlson, P. V.; Simmons, J. Q.; and Work, H. H.

"Emotional Problems of the Adoptee," *Archives of General Psychiatry*, 10:109–118, 1964.

The Single Parent. Parents Without Partners, Inc., 7910 Woodmont Avenue, Washington, D. C. 20014.

Smith, W. C. *The Stepchild.* Chicago: University of Chicago Press, 1953.

Snell, John E., Rosenwald, Richard J., and Robey, Ames. "The Wifebeater's Wife," *Archives of General Psychiatry*, 11: 107–112, 1964.

Solow, Robert A. "Psychological Aspects of Muscular Dystrophy," *Exceptional Children*, 32:99–163, 1965.

Stern, Edith M., and Castendyck, Elsa. *Care of the Handicapped Child*, New York: A. A. Wyn, 1950.

Van Der Veen, F.; Heubner, B.; Jorgens, B.; et al. "Relationships Between the Parents' Concept of the Family and Family Adjustment," *American Journal of Orthopsychiatry*, 34:45–55, 1964.

INDEX

GAP COMMITTEES, MEMBERS, AND OFFICERS

(as of January 1, 1973)

COMMITTEES

ADOLESCENCE

Joseph D. Noshpitz, Washington, D.C., *Chairman*
Warren J. Gadpaille, Englewood, Colo.
Charles A. Malone, Philadelphia, Pa.
Silvio J. Onesti, Jr., Boston, Mass.
Jeanne Spurlock, Nashville, Tenn.
Sidney L. Werkman, Denver, Colo.

AGING

Robert N. Butler, Washington, D.C., *Chairman*
Charles M. Gaitz, Houston, Tex.
Alvin I. Goldfarb, New York, N.Y.
Lawrence F. Greenleigh, Los Angeles, Calif.
Maurice E. Linden, Philadelphia, Pa.
Prescott W. Thompson, San Jose, Calif.
Montague Ullman, Brooklyn, N.Y.
Jack Weinberg, Chicago, Ill.

CHILD PSYCHIATRY

Joseph M. Green, Tucson, Ariz., *Chairman*

E. James Anthony, St. Louis, Mo.
James M. Bell, Canaan, N.Y.
Harlow Donald Dunton, New York, N.Y.
John F. Kenward, Chicago, Ill.
John F. McDermott, Jr., Honolulu, Hawaii
Exie E. Welsch, New York, N.Y.
Virginia N. Wilking, New York, N.Y.

THE COLLEGE STUDENT

Robert L. Arnstein, New Haven, Conn., *Chairman*
Harrison P. Eddy, New York, N.Y.
Malkah Tolpin Notman, Brookline, Mass.
Gloria C. Onque, Pittsburgh, Pa.
Kent E. Robinson, Towson, Md.
Earle Silber, Chevy Chase, Md.
Tom G. Stauffer, White Plains, N.Y.

THE FAMILY

Joseph Satten, San Francisco, Calif., *Chairman*
C. Christian Beels, Bronx, N.Y.

153

Ivan Boszormenyi-Nagy, Philadelphia, Pa.
Murray Bowen, Chevy Chase, Md.
Henry U. Grunebaum, Boston, Mass.
Margaret M. Lawrence, Pomona, N.Y.
Henry D. Lederer, Washington, D.C.
David Mendell, Houston, Tex.
Norman L. Paul, Cambridge, Mass.
Kurt O. Schlesinger, San Francisco, Calif.
Israel Zwerling, Bronx, N.Y.

GOVERNMENTAL AGENCIES
Paul Chodoff, Washington, D.C., *Chairman*
William S. Allerton, Richmond, Va.
Albert M. Biele, Philadelphia, Pa.
Sidney S. Goldensohn, New York, N.Y.
John E. Nardini, Washington, D.C.
Donald B. Peterson, Fulton, Mo.
Harvey L. P. Resnik, Chevy Chase, Md.
Harold Rosen, Baltimore, Md.

INTERNATIONAL RELATIONS
Bryant M. Wedge, Washington, D.C., *Chairman*
Francis F. Barnes, Chevy Chase, Md.
Eric A. Baum, Cambridge, Mass.
Eugene B. Brody, Baltimore, Md.
William D. Davidson, Washington, D.C.
Alexander Gralnick, Port Chester, N.Y.
Rita R. Rogers, Torrance, Calif.
Bertram H. Schaffner, New York, N.Y.

Mottram P. Torre, New Orleans, La.
Ronald M. Wintrob, Hartford, Conn.

MEDICAL EDUCATION
David R. Hawkins, Charlottesville, Va., *Chairman*
Robert S. Daniels, Cincinnati, Ohio
Raymond Feldman, Boulder, Colo.
Saul I. Harrison, Ann Arbor, Mich.
Harold I. Lief, Philadelphia, Pa.
John E. Mack, Boston, Mass.
William L. Peltz, Longview, Vt.
David S. Sanders, Los Angeles, Calif.
Robert A. Senescu, Albuquerque, N.M.
Roy M. Whitman, Cincinnati, Ohio

MENTAL HEALTH SERVICES
Merrill T. Eaton, Omaha, Nebr., *Chairman*
Allan Beigel, Tucson, Ariz.
H. Keith H. Brodie, Menlo Park, Calif.
Eugene M. Caffey, Jr., Washington, D.C.
Archie R. Foley, New York, N.Y.
James B. Funkhouser, Richmond, Va.
Robert S. Garber, Belle Mead, N.J.
Stanley Hammons, Frankfort, Ky.
Alan I. Levenson, Tucson, Ariz.
W. Walter Menninger, Topeka, Kans.
Donald Scherl, Boston, Mass.
Perry C. Talkington, Dallas, Tex.
Jack A. Wolford, Pittsburgh, Pa.

MENTAL RETARDATION
Henry H. Work, Washington, D.C., *Chairman*
Howard V. Bair, Parsons, Kans.

154

Stuart M. Finch, Ann Arbor, Mich.
Leo Madow, Philadelphia, Pa.
George Tarjan, Los Angeles, Calif.
Warren T. Vaughan, Jr., Burlingame, Calif.
Thomas G. Webster, Rockville, Md.

PREVENTIVE PSYCHIATRY
Stephen Fleck, New Haven, Conn., *Chairman*
Frederick Gottlieb, Sherman Oaks, Calif.
Benjamin Jeffries, Harper Woods, Mich.
Ruth W. Lidz, Woodbridge, Conn.
E. James Lieberman, Washington, D.C.
Mary E. Mercer, Nyack, N.Y.
Harris B. Peck, Bronx, N.Y.
Marvin E. Perkins, White Plains, N.Y.

PSYCHIATRY AND LAW
Carl P. Malmquist, Minneapolis, Minn., *Chairman*
Edward T. Auer, St. Louis, Mo.
John Donnelly, Hartford, Conn.
Peter B. Hoffman, Charlottesville, Va.
A. Louis McGarry, Brookline, Mass.
Seymour Pollack, Los Angeles, Calif.
Alan A. Stone, Cambridge, Mass.
Gene L. Usdin, New Orleans, La.

PSYCHIATRY AND RELIGION
Sidney S. Furst, New York, N.Y., *Chairman*
Stanley A. Leavy, New Haven, Conn.
Richard C. Lewis, New Haven, Conn.

Earl A. Loomis, Jr., New York, N.Y.
Albert J. Lubin, Woodside, Calif.
Mortimer Ostow, New York, N.Y.
Bernard L. Pacella, New York, N.Y.
Michael R. Zales, Greenwich, Conn.

PSYCHIATRY AND SOCIAL WORK
John A. MacLeod, Cincinnati, Ohio, *Chairman*
C. Knight Aldrich, Newark, N.J.
Maurice R. Friend, New York, N.Y.
Herbert C. Modlin, Topeka, Kans.
John C. Nemiah, Boston, Mass.
Alexander S. Rogawski, Los Angeles, Calif.
Charles B. Wilkinson, Kansas City, Mo.

PSYCHIATRY IN INDUSTRY
Clarence J. Rowe, St. Paul, Minn., *Chairman*
Spencer Bayles, Houston, Tex.
Thomas L. Brannick, Imola, Calif.
Duane Q. Hagen, St. Louis, Mo.
R. Edward Huffman, Asheville, N.C.
Herbert L. Klemme, Topeka, Kans.
Alan A. McLean, New York, N.Y.
David E. Morrison, Topeka, Kans.
John Wakefield, Cambridge, Mass.

PSYCHOPATHOLOGY
George E. Ruff, Philadelphia, Pa., *Chairman*
Wagner H. Bridger, New York, N.Y.
Sanford I. Cohen, Boston, Mass.
Daniel X. Freedman, Chicago, Ill.
Paul E. Huston, Iowa City, Iowa
Jack H. Mendelson, Boston, Mass.
Richard E. Renneker, Los Angeles, Calif

Grace Baker, New York, N.Y.

Walter E. Barton, Washington, D.C.

Anne R. Benjamin, Chicago, Ill.

Ivan C. Berlien, Coral Gables, Fla.

Sidney Berman, Washington, D.C.

Grete L. Bibring, Cambridge, Mass.

Edward G. Billings, Denver, Colo.

Carl A. L. Binger, Cambridge, Mass.

H. Waldo Bird, St. Louis, Mo.

Wilfred Bloomberg, Boston, Mass.

Peter W. Bowman, Pownal, Maine

Matthew Brody, Brooklyn, N.Y.

Ewald W. Busse, Durham, N.H.

Dale C. Cameron, Geneva, Switzerland

Norman Cameron, Tucson, Ariz.

Gerald Caplan, Boston, Mass.

Hugh T. Carmichael, Washington, D.C.

Morris E. Chafetz, Rockville, Md.

Jules V. Coleman, New Haven, Conn.

Robert Coles, Cambridge, Mass.

Harvey H. Corman, New York, N.Y.

Frank J. Curran, New York, N.Y.

Leonard J. Duhl, Berkeley, Calif.

Lloyd C. Elam, Nashville, Tenn.

Joel Elkes, Baltimore, Md.

Joseph T. English, New York, N.Y.

Louis C. English, Pomona, N.Y.

O. Spurgeon English, Narberth, Pa.

Jack R. Ewalt, Boston, Mass.

Dana L. Farnsworth, Boston, Mass.

Malcolm J. Farrell, Waverley, Mass.

Alfred Flarsheim, Chicago, Ill.

Alan Frank, Albuquerque, N.M.

Lawrence Z. Freedman, Chicago, Ill.

Moses M. Frohlich, Ann Arbor, Mich.

Daniel H. Funkenstein, Boston, Mass.

Albert J. Glass, Chicago, Ill.

Milton Greenblatt, Boston, Mass.

Maurice H. Greenhill, Scarsdale, N.Y.

John H. Greist, Indianapolis, Ind.

Roy R. Grinker, Sr., Chicago, Ill.

Ernest M. Gruenberg, Poughkeepsie, N.Y.

Joel S. Handler, Evanston, Ill.

Edward O. Harper, Washington, D.C.

Mary O'Neill Hawkins, New York, N.Y.

J. Cotter Hirschberg, Topeka, Kans.

Edward J. Hornick, New York, N.Y.

Joseph Hughes, Philadelphia, Pa.

Portia Bell Hume, Berkeley, Calif.

Lucie N. Jessner, Washington, D.C.

Irene M. Josselyn, Phoenix, Ariz.

Jay Katz, New Haven, Conn.

Sheppard G. Kellam, Chicago, Ill.

Marion E. Kenworthy, New York, N.Y.

Ernest W. Klatte, Santa Ana, Calif.

Othilda M. Krug, Cincinnati, Ohio

Zigmond M. Lebensohn, Washington, D.C.

P. Herbert Leiderman, Palo Alto, Calif.

Robert L. Leopold, Philadelphia, Pa.

David M. Levy, New York, N.Y.

Reginald S. Lourie, Washington, D.C.

Alfred O. Ludwig, Boston, Mass.

Jeptha R. MacFarlane, Westbury, N.Y.

Sidney G. Margolin, Denver, Colo.

Helen V. McLean, Chicago, Ill.

Karl A. Menninger, Topeka, Kans.

James G. Miller, Washington, D.C.

John A. P. Millet, New York, N.Y.

Kenneth J. Munden, Memphis, Tenn